EUROPEANS IN NORTH AMERICA

BEFORE COLUMBUS

MANDAN INDIANS
– THE "WHITE INDIANS," OF NORTH DAKOTA
THE WELSH CONNECTION
THE VIKING VISITORS

BY DR. DUANE R. LUND

Lund S&R Publications

Distributed By:
Adventure Publications
820 Cleveland • Cambridge, MN 55008

ISBN-10: 0-9740821-2-0
ISBN-13: 978-0-9740821-2-0

DEDICATION

To Pat (L. J.) Miller –
for the many photos he has contributed
to my books, especially covers,

To Don Droubie –
for the Mideast recipes he has contributed
to several of my cookbooks,

To Stan Edin –
for suggesting several of the subjects for my historical
research and the resulting books,

To Tony Walthall –
for his contributions to the layout and covers
of my earlier books and

To their wives,
Donna, Judy, Rose and Joey for putting up with the five
of us and our various ventures.

**We all have been special friends and neighbors on the Crow Wing River,
North of Staples, Minnesota, for more than thirty years.**

TABLE OF CONTENTS

CHAPTER ONE
THE MANDANS THE "WHITE INDIANS" OF NORTH DAKOTA

VISITS BY:

CHAPTER TWO
THE WELSH CONNECTION

CHAPTER THREE
THE VIKINGS

ADDENDUM

Chapter One

THE MANDANS
The "White Indians" of North Dakota

The Mandans are the best known of the North American Indian tribes thought to have inter-married with white Europeans before the time of Columbus. Neighboring Indian tribes were well aware that the Mandans were different, not only in the color of their skin, hair and eyes but also in their life style, the walled cities in which they lived, their houses, their work habits, how women were treated, the food they ate and more. They were regarded by some neighboring tribes as Europeans. The Assiniboin, a Sioux tribe, were quite certain they even knew which country they came from: France! By the time the United States had won its freedom and was organized as a country, it was known on the east cost that a colony of whites, or a tribe of white Indians, lived hundreds of miles inland. But the first white man to visit the Mandans was a French Canadian, Pierre La Verendrye.

Pierre La Verendrye

Pierre La Verendrye is not well know in the United States; his name is seldom – if ever – mentioned in American history texts. Yet, he was not only among the first but was also the most important explorer/trader to penetrate the continent. Radisson, Duluth, La Salle, Joliet, Marquette and others were ahead of him, and each contributed to the knowledge of the interior of North America, but La Verendrye was the dominant figure for a much longer period of time. He was "Commander of the Western Forts" from 1731 until his death in 1749. The others may have established a trading post for a season but La Verendrye was there for the long haul and he and his associates established seven more or less permanent forts – which also served as trading posts.

Pierre La Verendrye was born at Three Rivers, Quebec, in 1685. His father was governor of that settlement, and his mother was the daughter of a former governor, Pierre Boucher. Three Rivers was the "launching pad" for many of the explorations of that century, it is quite natural that a boy raised in this heroic atmosphere would turn his eyes to the still unknown areas of the West.

It was from Three Rivers that missionaries Breboeuf, Lalemant, Le Jeune, and Daniel began their journey which ended in martyrdom at the hands of the Mohawks.

It was from Three Rivers that Joliet and Marquette launched their explorations to the Great Lakes and Minnesota.

It was from Three Rivers that La Salle ventured toward Illinois.

It was from Three Rivers that the story came of young Radisson, a founder of the Hudson's Bay Company, who was carried away by the Iroquois at the age of sixteen, escaped, was recaptured, and was saved from a death of burning at the stake by an old Indian woman.

And it was from Three Rivers that De Noyon set forth to build a fort on Rainy River and make his mark in history as the first white man to see the Lake of the Woods, except from 1744 to 1747 when he asked to be relieved of that responsibility while he secured new financial support and mended his political fences.

For every explorer or priest associated with the Quebec village whose name is remembered in our history books, there were no doubt several others now long forgotten. Young La Verendrye must have known many of these men and heard firsthand their tales of success and failure, glory and hardship. As son of the governor, he was in a privileged position.

In an age when travel was often a hardship and always time consuming, La Verendrye saw a lot of the world. He joined the army at the age of twelve! He fought the British in Boston and the men of the Duke of Marlborough in Flanders. He suffered nine wounds and was left for dead on that foreign battlefield. On his return to Canada he was named Commander of a small trading post on the St. Maurice River. By 1727 he had earned a more responsible post on Lake Nipigon (Ontario). Not far from Nipigon was Fort Kiministiquia, west of which not much was known.

Apparently La Verendrye performed well, because only four years later he was named Commander of the Western Forts. He headquartered at Fort St. Charles, which he and his men constructed on the Northwest Angle of the Minnesota side of the Lake of the Woods. La Verendrye brought three of his sons with him: Jean Baptiste, Pierre and Francois. A fourth, his youngest, Louis-Joseph, joined the others later. His nephew, La Jemeraye, played a key role in developing additional forts and was actually second in command. Unfortunately he died, of natural causes, in the winter of 1735-36. In another tragedy, La Verendrye's oldest son, Jean Baptiste, and his priest, Father Alneau, along with nineteen soldier-voyagers, were murdered by a renegade band of Sioux of the prairies on an island in the Lake of the Woods as they were returning to Montreal for supplies.

**Artist conception of Jean Baptiste and Father Alman
leaving Fort St. Charles.**
Photo courtesy of the Minnesota Historical Society

LaVerendrye kept meticulous journals, most of which are in possession of the Champlain Society of Toronto and which were made available to this author along with several of his reports to The Marquis de Beauharnois, the then Governor General of Canada. These accounts tell in wondrous detail the adventures of the explorer and his sons, mostly on and around the Lake of the Woods. They may be found in two books by this author: "The Lake of the Woods Yesterday and Today" and "The Lake of the Woods, Earliest Accounts". for purposes of this book, only La Verendrye's references to the Mandans will be included.

Let us start with La Verendrye's report to the Governor General of Canada which covers the period between May 27,1733 and July 12, 1734 and in which we find his first mention of the Mandan Indians.

About half-way through the report, he speaks of a conference held at Fort St. Charles with representatives of three Cree and Three Assiniboin villages. Their spokesperson casually mentioned that they would not return until the next winter because in the spring they had promised to visit the Mandans to buy corn. Le Verendrye then wrote:

"When I heard the Mandans mentioned, I asked them several questions: I asked what they thought of the Mandans and whether they were savages like themselves. They replied that they took them to be French. They said their houses were much like ours except that the roofs were flat and covered with earth and stones. They live in forts made with double rows of posts and with two bastions in opposite corners. Their houses are large and are connected to the stockade so that one can make a tour of the fort on the tops of the houses. Their houses have cellars where Indian corn is kept in large wicker baskets. They never travel far from the fort. Both men and women[1] work in the fields.[1] Only the chiefs are excused from labor and they have servants to wait on them."

"We were further told that these barracks dwellers are very tall in stature, well proportioned, white, and walk with their toes turned out.[2] Their hair is said to be blonde or brown – and a few black. Some have full beards, some trim their beards, and others pull the hairs out. They are reported to be friendly and to receive strangers warmly, yet always seem to be on their guard. They do not visit the neighboring tribes. They clothe themselves in leather and in dressed skins which have been skillfully worked and are of many colors. They wear a kind of jacket with trousers and stockings of the same material. Their shoes and stockings are apparently of one piece of goods. The women are reported to be dressed in long gowns with a kind of tunic which goes down to the ankles.

[1] Indian men rarely performed such menial tasks.
[2] Most Indians walked with their toes turned in a bit.

They have girdles with aprons attached, both made of finely worked leather. their hair is braided and worn in coils on their heads."

"They went on to tell us that the tribe is very industrious. They sow considerable quantities of corn, beans, oats, and grains which they trade with their neighbors who come to their forts to get them. The women do not work as hard as the Indian women, but are more engaged in domestic affairs, keeping their homes neat and clean. When necessary, they help in the fields."

"The Mandans raise several kinds of animals such as horses and goats. They reportedly have domesticated fowls including turkeys, chickens, geese, ducks, and others which our Indians here did not recognize. Their most common food is Indian corn, just as it is with our French voyageurs. They eat quantities of meat such as buffalo, moose, deer, etc. These they trap in large pits covered with grass and twigs. They usually hunt on horseback in groups."

"I have forgotten to mention that their smaller forts are usually square measuring five or six arpents on each side,[1] and they are surrounded by a deep ditch. The stockade has a double gate. There is a large open space in the middle of the stockade and all the houses face this courtyard. All of their forts are constructed on the banks of rivers and each has an underground passage from the courtyard to the water's edge whereby they can embark on the river without being noticed. Their weapons, both offensive and defensive, are bow and arrow, buckler[2], axe, and lance."

"We were told that the home of the chief is very large and higher than all the rest; it occupies the whole side opposite from the gate. The chief's quarters and those of his servants or slaves are at one end; the middle is reserved for public gatherings and receptions, and the other end is assigned to the chief's wives. this house has three main doors. There is a pole planted in front of the chief's home topped by a weather vane. At the low ends of the house and raised above it are two buffalo heads with ornamental carvings (apparently the coat of arms of the tribe.)"

"This tribe has only one principal chief, but it has a number of forts on both banks of a great river which flows west.[3] the Assiniboin told me that they know of nine such forts, a league or less apart, but they have heard there are a great many

---

[1] The enclosure would be about 4-1/2 to 5 acres.
[2] Shield.
[3] The Missouri River, which actually flows south past the Mandan villages.

more both up and down stream from the one in which the principal chief resides. Each fort has its own chief, but each is subject to the first. When there is cause for alarm, they warn each other from bank to bank with trumpets, so that in a few hours the whole tribe is on the alert. They apparently have other means of signalling as well."

"We were further told that their canoes are small and made of skins. they are rounded at the ends and propelled by a single person with a double-bladed paddle or two short oars."

"This river is reportedly 18 to 20 arpents wide,[1] is very deep, has a good current, and abounds with fish. The Indians are not aware of any falls or rapids. It waters a vast, mountainless country, partly bare and prairie-like and partly wooded. The trees are tall and apparently similar to our eastern varieties, including oak."

"The same insects as we have in the East are found along the stream's banks. A snake is reported which is two to three feet long, more black than grey, and which has two horns on its head about the length of a finger. When it moves it holds its head erect and forward, but is not harmful unless attacked or stepped on. This tribe is supposed to have an herb which acts as an antidote to the snake's bite, so it is dreaded only by strangers entering the country."

"When I asked the orator if he could understand the language of the Mandans or knew their words for "fire", "water", etc., he said "no", and that even though his job with his own tribe is to act as an interpreter, he did not stay long enough to retain any words of their language. All he could say was that they speak and sing like the French, and that he believes the Mandans to be Frenchmen like us."[2]

---

[1] An arpent is .85 acres. The term also refers to the length of one side of the square arpent. Our acre is a square of 208'x208' or 43,264 square feet. An arpent would then be .85x43,264 or 36,774 square feet.

[2] A slave of the Cree who had originally been captured by the Assiniboin from this general area, told La Verendrye that there were numerous villages, some as large as two leagues across (five miles!). He also reported that the Indians there were good farmers, raising grain and fruits. Game is plentiful and the Indians there hunted them with bows and arrows. There were no canoes, because there was no bark, so the used boats made of animal skins (bull boats make of buffalo hides stretched over a light frame). Because there is little wood, the natives burned dried animal dung. He also reported that there was a tribe of dwarfs along the right bank of the Red River.

"I then asked the speaker if his people knew anything about the lower end of the river. He replied that the Mandans had been asked the same question, but they could not say, except that they were aware of no other tribes other than their own, but that their people's villages did not extend along the river as far as the sea."

"I asked next what special tools they might have with which to cut wood and cultivate the soil. He replied that they had none of the quality of ours but were pleased to exchange their corn for the axes,[1] knives, etc. which the Assiniboin brought them. The implements they made for themselves were made of a yellow metal harder than copper."

"Their knives, although of the same material, have staghorn handles and were reported to be very well made. Instead of metal pots they used vessels of clay and sandstone decorated on the outside with floral designs. the inside is finished with a kind of lacquer. Their household utensils are similarly made and they also use well made wicker baskets."

"I inquired further if the Mandans knew anything about us. The Assiniboin responded, "It is just over a year since we received your message which you sent in behalf of our Father. It made us so happy we told everyone we met. It is only four moons since we left the Mandans, so we did speak to them about the Frenchman and the message we had received in his name. They were so pleased, and their great chief said to us, 'You are going to see the French. I ask that you tell the chief from me that it would give me great pleasure to see him or any of his people, in order that we may become friends with them. If he comes himself or sends another, I beg him to let me know ahead of time so that I may send a party to meet him and give him the welcome he deserves."

"Before concluding the council, I told them it would be impossible for us to visit the Mandans in less than a year's time, because most of my men were going to Montreal for a new supply of trade goods to provide for the needs of all of the Indians of this area, for whom I felt sorry, and particularly to see our Father to let him know what has been going on here."

---

[1] The original manuscript has a note in the margin here: "Would not these be axes similar to those given in Peru by the Spaniards when it was discovered?"

"On June 4, I learned from one of our employees who had come from Maurepas that in the month of January a white-skinned Mandan had come disguised as an Assiniboin Indian.

He asked permission to sleep in the fort, saying that he was not a savage like the rest. My nephew, however, being quite ill, was not notified. The man who was assigned the duty of closing the gate, either because he did not understand the language or out of carelessness, put him out that night with the rest of the Indians. He didn't report the incident until several days after the Mandan Indian had left, a fact which I regret very much."

In La Verendye's report to the governor for the year 1737, he again mentions the Mandans:

"I asked the Assiniboin where they intended to spend the summer. they replied they intended to go to the country of the Mandans. They would trade axes, knives, fire-steels and other items for Indian corn and beans. I decided to entrust them with the gift I had brought for that tribe. They promised to deliver the gift as well as the following message in your name:

1. That the French desire to establish friendship with the Mandans and to carry on trade with them, and

2. That we invite them to come in the fall to the fork of the Red River where we intend to build a fort so that we may be nearer to them."

On October 9, 1738, La Verendrye set out from Fort St. Charles with an unknown number of his men and a whole village of Assiniboin. Let us let La Verendrye pick up the story here.

"Every day they (the Assiniboin) talked to us about the whites we were about to see. They said they were Frenchmen like ourselves, who said they were descended from us. Everything they told us gave us hope of making a truly remarkable discovery. As we went along, M. de Lamarque and I speculated as to what we might say to these people; we believed all that the Assiniboin had told us. Later, we would learn that we should have discounted their claims considerably."

"I called M. de Lamarque's attention to the formation in which the Assiniboin marched in order to avoid surprise attack. From the very first mountain the whole country was a prairie, but with frequent hills and valleys which made us very tired after climbing up and down several times each day. There were some magnificent flat plains, however, some three or four leagues in extent. The marching order of the Assiniboin villagers, especially when they are in large numbers, is in three columns; the scouts in front, the wings extending back as a good rear guard, and the old and disabled marching in the main body, which is in the middle. I had all the Frenchmen stay together as much as possible. If the scouts see any herds of buffalo along the way, as often happens, they raise a cry, which is easily heard by the rear guard. All of the most active men in the columns then join the vanguard and surround the animals. After killing a number of them, each man takes what meat he wants. Since the hunt stops the march, the vanguard marks out a campground and no one is allowed to go farther. The women and the dogs carry all the baggage. The men carry only their weapons. They often even make their dogs carry firewood, as they frequently have to camp out on the prairie where clumps of trees are sometimes far apart."

"On the morning of October 28th, we arrived at the place where we were supposed to meet the delegation of Mandans. They arrived that evening, one chief with thirty of his men and four Assiniboin. After studying our village for sometime from a height of ground (and the village was pretty large) he came down and I had him escorted into my lodge and invited him to sit down in a place which has been prepared for him – next to me. He took the seat and others of his tribe joined him. He then presented me with some Indian corn – still on the cob – and a roll of their tobacco. The tobacco was not good, because they do not know how to prepare it. Although it is a good deal like ours, they do not plant it (it grows wild) and they cut it while it is still green, using the stalks and leaves together."

"I confess I was greatly surprised, since I was expecting to see a people quite different from the other Indians, from the stories the Assiniboin had told us. They do not differ much from the Assiniboin, being naked except for a buffalo hide worn rather carelessly and without a breech cloth. I knew then that I would have to discount a great deal of what the Assiniboin had told me. The chief spoke Assiniboin (which was then translated to French) and he told me of the joy which my arrival brought to his people. He asked me to receive them as your children. He wished his people in the future to be united with us. He said that all he had was at my disposal. He invited me to stay at his fort which, though smaller than the rest, was the nearest and well-stocked with provisions. There were six forts in all, he said, belonging to the same tribe; his was the only one that was not on the river. He said

that he had always hoped to see me, and that when we arrived at his village, he would show me the two collars I had sent him earlier.[1]**"**

La Verendrye tells us that the Mandan Chief was overwhelmed with the size of the Assiniboin village (probably well over 1000) and was concerned about feeding so many people. He cleverly let it be know that he was worried about the trip back to his fort because Sioux were in the area. After a lengthy discussion, the Assiniboin decided to leave the main village there and just send a band of warriors on as an escort for La Verendrye. His ruse had worked. The Chief knew he would still be able to trade with the Assiniboin and would give them corn, tobacco, skins, and colored plumes in exchange for guns, axes, kettles, powder, bullets, knives, and awls (which they in turn had received from the French). La Verendrye and later explorers were impressed with the business ability of the Mandans and said that they took particular advantage of the Assiniboin.

Perhaps it is well to note that the Assiniboin, through a relatively gentle and peace-loving tribe, were looked down upon by their neighbors. Although numerous, they were not considered to be good fighters or particularly brave. They were not thought of as being particularly bright. The Cree leadership, when they learned La Verendrye would be traveling with the Assiniboin, said they "hoped he could sharpen their wits". Although a Sioux people themselves, they were very much afraid of the Sioux of both the Prairies and the Woodlands. They also had a rather strange habit of crying on most any formal occasion; they became known, therefore, to early whites as "the weepers".

We'll let La Verendrye pick up the story once again:

"We left on the morning of the 30th, about 600 men and several women without children, the best walkers. On the evening of the third day of the march, while we were still about seven leagues from the first fort of the Mandans, I was told that one of the Assiniboin had stolen my box which contained my papers and other important items.

The Indian had taken it from my slave, who was carrying it, on the pretext of relieving him for awhile. I immediately sent two men back to catch him. I learned later that they did rescue my box, but because of their fear of the Sioux, remained with the other villagers until my return. As a result, I was deprived of many things of which I was in need every day."

---

[1] The ceremonial collar contained bead work and had trade value. It was very similar to the bead belts used for trade by other tribes. It was sometimes called "wampum".

"The orator gave notice that we should be prepared to leave before four o'clock the next morning in order to arrive at a convenient time at the fort. About noon, after going about a league and a half, we found a number of people who had come to meet us gathered by a stream. They had lighted a fire while waiting and had brought along some food for us to eat, which included cooked grain and flour worked into a paste with pumpkin. The chiefs had prepared a place for me near the fire, but first they gave me a pipe and some food. M. de Lamarque arrived a short time later. I asked him to sit down beside me and eat while resting. After resting two full hours, we were told it was time to move on. I had one of my sons take the flag showing the colors of the arms of France and march at the head of the procession. The other Frenchmen were ordered to follow in proper marching order. The Sieur Nolan relieved my son by taking turns with him in carrying the flag. The Mandans would not let me walk; they offered to carry me. The Assiniboin advised me that I would hurt their feelings if I rejected their offer, so I let them carry me the rest of the way."

"At four arpents from the fort, on a little hill, the elders of the tribe, along with a large band of younger men, were waiting to present me with a pipe and to show me the two collars I had sent them previously. They gave seats to me and M. de Lamarque. I accepted their compliments and expressions of joy at my arrival. I ordered my son, the Chevalier, to draw the French up in line with the standard four paces in front. All of the Assiniboin who had guns fell in behind the Frenchmen. Upon the conclusion of the exchange of compliments, I ordered a salute to the fort of three volleys. A great many people had come to meet us, but that was nothing compared to the numbers we saw along the rampart and along the ditches. I marched the men in good order to the fort, which I entered at four o'clock in the afternoon on December 3, escorted by all the French and the Assiniboin. I was let into the lodge of the chief. It was large, but not big enough to hold all the people who wanted to enter. The crowd was so large that the Assiniboin and the Mandans were stepping on each others' heels. The only open space was where we were, myself, M. de Lamarque, his brother, and my sons. I requested that some be asked to leave to make room for my Frenchmen so that they could put down their luggage in a safe place.

I told them that everyone would have plenty of opportunities to see me. The place was cleared, but not soon enough: someone had already stolen the bag which contained my gifts. It was really the fault of one of my hired men who, without thinking, had set the bag down in the great crowd and had not stayed close to it."

La Verendrye was embarrassed not to have gifts to present his hosts, but they understood, knowing what had happened. In fact, the Assiniboin and the Mandans began blaming each other for the theft. The Mandans proved to be generous hosts and put everything at the disposal of the Frenchmen.

When La Verendrye indicated that he planned to stay for quite some time, the Mandans expressed great joy. The Assiniboin then indicated that they wanted to return to the other villagers just as soon as they had completed their trading and would wait there for La Verendrye. However, the trading having been completed, the Assiniboin showed no signs of leaving. The wily Mandans then reported that their scouts had seen Sioux Indians heading that way. The Assiniboin quickly departed, leaving only five of their number as guides for La Verendrye's return.

The Mandans made a formal request that La Verendrye accept them as children of the French. He responded by placing his hands on the head of each chief as a symbol of adoption. He said that "they responded with shouts of joy and appreciation".

Unfortunately, when the Assiniboin left, La Verendrye's interpreter went with them. He was in love with one of the young women who had made the trip to the Mandan fort. When she insisted on going back to the other villagers with the departing Assiniboin, he followed. This was a serious deterrent to the explorer's plans. He then had to learn by what he saw and could no longer ask questions.

La Verendrye did learn, however, that other tribes were along the river further south. Among them were the "Panana" and the "Pananis" – probably the Pawnee. He also learned that still farther south were the Spanish. He was led to believe that the Mandans themselves had seen them.[1] He was also told that since the Spanish wore armor, they could not be harmed by arrows. But the Indians had learned that by killing the horse, the rider was at their mercy, since they could not run because of the heavy armor. La Verendrye sent his son, the Chevalier, with Nolan and six other Frenchmen to visit the nearest village, which was on the Missouri River. When they returned, they reported that they had been very well received and that the second village was much bigger than the first.

They had been told that the fort farthest away (nearest the Pawnee) was the largest of all. They were impressed how clean and well kept the streets of the village were.

---

[1] It is possible that the Spanish did some trading with the Mandans and may have visited their southern most villages.

While they were gone, La Verendrye and de Lamarque toured the first village; here is the explorer's description:

"I gave orders to count the cabins, and we found that there were about one hundred and thirty. All the streets, squares, and dwellings are uniform in appearance. They look so much alike, the Frenchmen often lose their way as they move about the village. They keep the streets and open areas very clean. The ramparts are smooth and wide. The palisade is supported on cross pieces, morticed into posts fifteen feet apart. The walls of the city are lined on the inside with green buffalo hides suspended from the top. There were four bastions (towers). The fort is built on an elevation out in the prairie and is surrounded by a ditch fifteen feet deep and fifteen to eighteen feet wide. The entrances to the fort may be reached only by wooden steps; these can be raised up into the fort in times of attack. If all their forts are like this, it could be said that they are impregnable to other tribes. Indeed, there is nothing primitive about the fortifications.[1]"

"This tribe is of mixed blood, white and Indian. The women are rather handsome, particularly those with light complexions. They have an abundance of blond hair. The whole tribe, both men and women, is very industrious. Their homes are large and spacious, divided into several rooms by wide boards."

Nothing is left lying about; all their belongings are placed in bags and hung on posts. Their beds are enclosed by skins. They all go to bed naked; both the men and the women. Many of the women even go about the village naked, except for a narrow loin-cloth about a hand-wide and a foot long, fastened to a girdle – in front only. All of the women wear this kind of protection, even when they are wearing a petticoat or other garments, so that they are not embarrassed when they sit down, and they do not have to keep their thighs closed as other Indian women do."

"The roebuck (antelope) is plentiful in the region; it is of a very small variety. Their fort is well provided with cellars, where they store all they have in the way of grains, meat, fat, dressed skins, and bear skins. They have a great stock of these things, which form the currency of the country. The more they have, the richer they consider themselves. They are very fond of tattooing, but neither men nor women have more than half their bodies decorated. They do very fine wicker work, both in basket and flat forms."

---

[1] Later white explorers believed the fortifications had been built or at least engineered by earlier white visitors.

La Verendrye also noted that the men were tall and well built.[1] He said that the Mandans were fond of feasts and had a great variety of dishes; as many as twenty were served him in a single day. He identified some as being made of corn, beechnut, and pumpkin. He also spoke of their great use of sunflower seeds. The men were also fond of sports and games. La Verendrye learned that the Mandans had smaller, "summer forts" of about fifty dwellings each, nearer their farm plots.

Handicapped by the loss of his interpreter and feeling that there was little more to be learned, La Verendrye decided to leave the Mandans in December and return to the Assiniboin. On the 8th of that month he sent an advance contingent of two Frenchmen and two Assiniboin to alert the village to their coming. He left behind one of M. de Lamarque's men and his own personal servant to spend the rest of the winter trying to learn the language.

Although La Verendrye did not return to the Mandans, two of his sons did.

The temptation is just too great to not mention here reference a Swedish traveler, Peter Kalm, made to an object he said La Verendrye told him he picked up in his travels. It was a rock on which had been inscribed certain letters in an unknown language. The rock was reportedly about "one foot in length and four or five inches wide". It was fixed onto a pillar and La Verendrye's men supposedly broke it off. La Verendrye is also quoted by Kalm as telling of other pillars, apparently man-made, found here and there in the wilderness, but without any inscriptions. He supposedly told Kalm that he brought the stone back east and gave to the Jesuits.

They are said to have thought the alphabet to be Tartaric. Kalm further reported that the rock was eventually sent to France.

Theodore Blegen, the late Minnesota historian and Dean of the Graduate School of the Univeristy of Minnesota, enjoyed speculating that this rock, if indeed it did exist, could have been picked up in the country of the Mandans. He further pointed out that Tartaric lettering and the runic symbols of the Vikings could not be told apart except by experts. Blegen then teased us with the question, "Could the white blood of the Mandans have been Viking blood?"

---

[1] Later visitors described the Mandan men as "not very tall". Could it be that the taller ones died in the plague which occurred between La Verendrye's visit and that of George Catlin?

Unfortunately, the mysterious rock has never been found, although efforts have been made over the years to verify its existence. It is also strange that La Verendrye never mentioned the rock in any of his letters or journals which have survived.

As we have seen, La Verendrye was quite disappointed in what he found among the Mandan people. His Indian contacts had given him such high hopes that he was about to discover a lost French colony, he possibly failed to recognize how significant the differences were between these people and the other Indian tribes. After all, much of what the Assiniboin and others had told him was true. They settled in cities rather than roaming in nomadic fashions like so many tribes. The cities themselves were unusual in that they had walls (stockades) and ditches (moats)[1] around them for protection. Their dwellings were more house-like than those of other tribes and they were separated by streets. The male and female roles were more European, with men working in fields along side women and walking side by side instead of the man ahead of the wife. And, perhaps most significant, were the light colored skins, blue and hazel eyes and hair every color but red characterizing a significant number of Mandans. La Verendrye did conclude that "the tribe is of mixed blood, Indian and white".

As we have said, two of La Verendrye's sons, Louis Joseph and Francois, returned to the Mandans in 1742 and engaged two Mandan guides. their purpose was to find the Western Sea, but they went no farther than the mountains. There has been much debate as to just how far the young La Verendryes did explore. After weighing all the writings, it appears safest to say that they went at least as far as the Black Hills, but perhaps no farther.

One of the most interesting footnotes to the La Verendrye sons' western explorations is a lead tablet[2] they left to mark their presence in that country. It bore the following inscription, in Latin:

ANNO XXVI REGNI LUDOVICI XV PROREGE…
ILLVSTRISSIMO DOMINO DOMINO MARCHIONE…
DE BEAVHARNOIS M.D.CC.XXXXI…
PETRVS TGAVLTIER DE LAVERENDRIE POSVIT…

---

[1] Sometimes the moats were inside the walls of the city and dry, more like ditches. During an attack, Mandan warriors would lie in them and shoot through holes in the walls cut close to the ground.

[2] Pierre La Verendrye had left a similar plate in a box with the Mandans during his stay with them. It has not been found.

On the reverse side of the tablet was scratched the burial date, "March 30, 1743", and the names of two witnesses, "A. Miotte" and either "Louy la Londette" or "Laudette". The men were no doubt part of the La Verendrye crew. Unfortunately, the La Verendryes and other early explorers seldom recorded the names of their men. Pierre La Verendrye often neglected even to indicate which of his sons he was talking about.

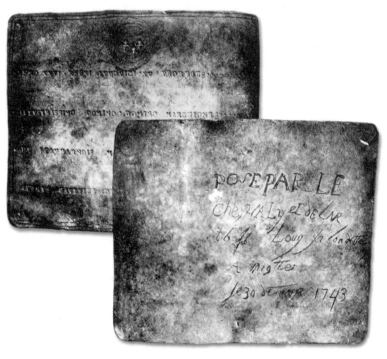

Front side of the metal plaque   **Reverse side of the metal plaque.**
Photo courtesy of the Minnesota Historical Society

The young La Verendryes recorded in their journal that the tablet was burried on a hill by the Missouri River under a pylon of rocks.

On February 16, 1913, some school children accidentally came upon the lead plate. They found it on a hill, near Pierre, South Dakota, but the rock structure had apparently been scattered long before. Truly an exciting discovery!

LEWIS AND CLARK

Now let us leave the La Verendryes and the year 1738 and fast-forward 66 years to 1804. Lewis and Clark spent the first winter of their historic expedition with the Mandans and the neighboring Gros Ventres (Big Billies). They built a fort with a stockade (they were concerned about the various Sioux tribes that inhabited what is now North Dakota) which enclosed comfortable housing and work shops. Appropriately, they named it "Fort Mandan".

The Mandans had a number of visitors during those intervening years, but those visitors kept few records and what they had to say pretty much echoed La Verendrye's journals, describing the tribe as part white, industrious, living in walled cities and relatively nice homes, good farmers, etc. Because of their reputation, most explorers visited the Mandans. John McDonnell, in his "Account of the Red River", characterized the tribe as "the best husbandmen in the whole Northwest" and as excellent farmers. He also called them "the mildest and most honest Indians of the whole continent".

When Lewis and Clark arrived in 1804, they found several traders in residence who worked for the French North West Company. Employees of the Hudson's Bay Company also called on the Mandans.

The big difference between the tribe in 1738 and in 1805 was the huge reduction in numbers. The nine villages that existed at the time of La Verendrye's visit had been reduced to only two. La Verendrye did not estimate the total population but Lewis and Clark thought there were fewer than 2,000 inhabitants in the two villages combined when they were there. The endless war with the Sioux tribes accounted for much of the decline but the smallpox epidemic of 1782 had an even greater impact. Another change was that the tribe, in the interim, had moved about sixty miles upstream, probably to get away from the larger concentrations and migrations of the Sioux.

Although Lewis and Clark and other members of their expedition kept meticulous journals, they said relatively little about the Mandans in contrast to the detailed descriptions of La Verendrye and George Catlin (whose letters will follow). Lewis and Clark said nothing to contradict the descriptions of the other visitors but referred to the unique features of the Mandans in a rather incidental or in an off-hand way. For example, Clark described a prairie fire that burned to death a man and woman and severely injured others, including "a boy half white who was saved unhurt in the midst of the flames. These ignorant people said he was saved by the Great Medicine Spirit because he was white". Lewis and Clark did conclude that the Mandans were, without a doubt, part white.

Sacajawea, the Native American woman who acted as an interpreter with some of the western tribes, joined the expedition here. She has become nearly as well know as Lewis and Clark. There is an interesting note in Lewis' diary for February 11, 1805:

"About five o'clock this evening one of the wives of Charbono[1] (Sacajawea) was delivered of a fine boy. It is worthy to remark that this was the first child which this woman had born, and as is common in such cases her labour was tedious and the pain violent. Mr. Jessome informed me that he frequently had administered a small portion of the rattle of a rattle snake, which he assured me had never failed to produce the desired effect, that of hastening the birth of the child; having the rattle of a snake by me I gave it to him and he administered two rings of it to the woman, broken into small pieces with the fingers and added to a small quantity of water. Whether this medicine was truly the cause or not I shall not undertake to determine, but I was informed that she had not taken it more than ten minutes before she brought forth."

The boy was named "Jean Baptiste" (the father was at least part French). Sacajawea died in 1812 of a "putrid fever" when the boy was seven and a second son, Lisette, was only four months old. Clark adopted the two boys and saw to their education. We don't know what happened to Lisette, but Jean Baptiste later traveled to Europe where he spent six years. After he returned he worked as a trapper with Kit Carson.

Now let us fast forward once again, this time to the year 1832 and hear from another distinguished visitor of the Mandans:

GEORGE CATLIN

Catlin has given us extraordinary descriptions of the American Indians of the 1830s, both in his published letters and in his hundreds of paintings and sketches. He visited most of the western tribes between 1830 and 1836. He lived with the Mandans in 1832-33 and spent more time with them than any other tribe – a good indication of how fascinated he was by these remarkable people.

George Catlin was the fifth of fourteen children. He was born in Wilkes-Barre, Pennsylvania, in 1796. He was well educated and worked briefly as an attorney, but his true love was art. He earned a good reputation as a portrait painter, unfortunately

[1] One of the guides.

he was unable to earn much money. His work was good, but apparently Americans of that era just weren't all that interested in Indians. He published his letters describing American Indians in Europe where there was more interest, but this did not earn him much money either. Eventually, in 1852, Catlin went bankrupt. Were he alive today, his paintings, which are on display in some of the nation's most prestigious museums and galleries, would have made him a very wealthy man.

Catlin met William Clark in 1830 and traveled briefly with him. From Clark he heard about the Mandans and their many unique characteristics, including the fact they were part white.

Sixteen of Catlin's published letters (or chapters) about North American Indians were about the Mandans. We shall reproduce here the two letters which best describe the tribe, but will also add his description of the demise of the tribe. We have left the spelling and grammar just as written by Catlin. Since he was a well educated man we can only assume both were correct in that day.

LETTER NO. 11 FROM GEORGE CATLIN'S BOOK, "LETTERS AND NOTES ON THE MANNERS, CUSTOMS, AND CONDITIONS OF THE NORTH AMERICAN INDIANS" (FIRST PUBLISHED IN LONDON, ENGLAND, IN 1844)

MANDAN VILLAGE, UPPER MISSOURI

George Catlin

"I said that I was here in the midst of a strange people, which is literally true; and I find myself surrounded by subjects and scenes worthy of the pens of Irving or Cooper – of the Pencils of Raphael or Hogarth; rich in legends and romances, which would require no aid of the imagination for a book or a picture."

"The Mandans (or See-pohs-kah-nu-mah-kah-kee, "people of the pheasants[1]," as they call themselves), are perhaps one of the most ancient tribes of Indians in our country. Their origin, like that of all other tribes is from necessity, involved in mystery and obscurity. Their traditions and peculiarities I shall casually recite in this or future epistles; which when understood, will at once, I

---

[1] These birds were not the pheasants we know today, which were imported from China in more modern times. It probably refers to prairie chickens or sharptail grouse.

...ink, denominate them a peculiar and distinct race. They take great pride in relating their traditions, with regard to their origin; contending that they were the first people created on earth. Their existence in these regions has not been from a very ancient period; and, from what I could learn of their traditions, they have, at a former period, been a very numerous and powerful nation; but by the continual wars which have existed between them and their neighbours, they have been reduced to their present numbers.

"This tribe is at present located on the west bank of the Missouri, about 1800 miles above St. Louis, and 200 below the mouth of Yellow Stone River. They have two villages only, which are about two miles distant from each other; and number in all (as near as I can learn), about 2000 souls. their present villages are beautifully located, and judiciously also, for defense against the assaults of their enemies. The site of the lower (or principal) town, in particular, is one of the most beautiful and pleasing that can be seen in the world, and even more beautiful than imagination could ever create. In the very midst of an extensive valley (embraced within a thousand graceful swells and parapets or mounds of interminable green, changing to blue, as they vanish in distance) is built the city, or principal town of the Mandans. On an extensive plain (which is covered with a green turf, as well as the hills and dales, as far as the eye can possibly range, without tree or bush to be seen) are to be seen rising from the ground, and toward the heavens, domes – (not "of gold" but of dirt) – and the thousand spears (not "spires") and scalp-poles, of the semi-subterraneous village of the hospitable and gentlemanly Mandans. These people formerly (and within the recollection of may of their oldest men) lived fifteen or twenty miles farther down the river, in ten contiguous villages; the marks or runes of which are yet plainly to be seen. At that period, it is evident, as well from the number of lodges which their villages contained, as from their traditions, that their numbers were much greater than at the present day."

"There are other, and very interesting, traditions and historical facts relative to a still prior location and condition of these people, of which I shall speak more fully on a future occasion. From these, when they are promulgated, I think there may be a pretty fair deduction drawn, that they formerly occupied the lower part of the Missouri, and even the Ohio and Muskingum, and have gradually made their way up the Missouri to where they now are."

"There are many remains on the river below this place (and, in fact, to be seen nearly as low down as St. Louis), which show clearly the peculiar construction of Mandan lodges, and consequently carry a strong proof of the above position. While descending the river, however, which I shall commence in a few weeks, in a canoe, this will be a subject of interest; and I shall give it close examination."

"The ground on which the Mandan village is at present built, was admirably selected for defense; being on a bank forty or fifty feet above. The greater part of this bank is nearly perpendicular, and of solid rock. The river, suddenly changing its course to a right-angle, protects two sides of the village, which is built upon this promontory or angle; they have therefore but one side to protect, which is effectually done by a strong piquet, and a ditch inside of it, three or four feet in depth. The piquet is composed of timbers of a foot or more in diameter and eighteen feet high, set firmly in the ground at sufficient distances from each other to admit guns and other missiles to be fired between them. The ditch (unlike that of civilized modes of fortification) is inside of the piquet, in which their warriors screen their bodies from the view and weapons of their enemies, whilst they are reloading and discharging their weapons through the piquets."

"The Mandans are undoubtedly secure in their villages, from the attacks of any Indian nation, and have nothing to fear, except when they meet their enemy on the prairie. Their village has a most novel appearance to the eye of a stranger; their lodges are closely grouped together leaving but just room enough for walking and riding between them; and appear from without to be built entirely of dirt; but one is surprised when he enters them, to see the neatness, comfort, and spacious dimensions of these earth-covered dwellings. They all have a circular form, and are from forty to sixty feet in diameter. Their foundations are prepared by digging some two feet in the ground, and forming the door of earth, by leveling the requisite size for the lodge. These floors or foundations are all perfectly circular, and varying in size in proportion to the number of inmates, or of the quality or standing of the families which are to occupy them. The superstructure is then produced, by arranging, inside of this circular excavation, firmly fixed in the ground and resting against the bank, a barrier or wall of timbers, some eight or nine inches in diameter, of equal height (about six feet) placed on end, and resting against each other, supported by a formidable embankment of earth raised against them outside; then, resting upon the tops of these timbers or poles, are others of equal size and equal in numbers, of twenty or twenty-five feet in length, resting firmly against each other, and sending their upper or small ends towards the centre and top of the lodge; rising at an angle of forty-five degrees to the apex or sky-light, which is about three or four feet in diameter, answering as a chimney and a sky-light at the same time. The roof of the lodge being thus formed, is supported by beams passing around the inner part of the lodge about the middle of these poles or timbers, and themselves upheld by four or five large posts passing down to the floor of the lodge. On the top of, and over the poles forming the roof, is placed a complete mat of willow-boughs, of half a foot or more in thickness, which protects the timbers from the dampness of the earth, with which the lodge is covered from bottom to top, to the depth of two or three feet; and then with a hard or tough clay, which is impervious to water, and which with long use becomes quite hard, and a lounging place for the whole family in pleasant weather – for sage – for wooing lovers – for dogs and all; an airing place – a look-out – a place for gossip and mirth – a seat for the solitary gaze and mediations of the stern warrior, who sits and contemplates the peaceful mirth and happiness that is breathed beneath him, fruits of his hard-fought battles, on fields of desperate combat with bristling Red Men."

"The floors of these dwellings are of earth, but so hardened by use, and swept so clean, and tracked by bare and moccasined feet, that they have almost a polish, and would scarcely soil the whitest linen. In the centre, and immediately under the sky-light is the fireplace – a hole of four or five feet in diameter, of a circular form, sunk a foot or more below the surface, and curbed around with stone. Over the fireplace, and suspended from the apex of diverging props or poles, is generally seen the pot or kettle, filled with buffalo meat; and around it are the family, reclining in all the most picturesque attitudes and groups, resting on their buffalo-robes and beautiful mats of rushes. These cabins are so spacious, that they hold from twenty to forty persons – a family and all their connexions. They all sleep on bedsteads similar in form to ours, but generally not quite so high; made of round poles rudely lashed together with thongs. A buffalo skin, fresh stripped from the animal, is stretched across the bottom poles, and about two feet from the floor; which, when it dries, becomes much contracted, and forms a perfect sacking-bottom. The fur side of this skin is placed uppermost, on which they lie with great comfort, with a buffalo-robe folded for a pillow, and others drawn over them instead of blankets. These beds, as far as I have seen them (and I have visited almost every lodge in the village), are uniformly screened with a covering of buffalo or elk skins, oftentimes beautifully dressed and placed over the upright poles or frame, like a suit of curtains; leaving a hole in front, sufficiently spacious for the occupant to pass in and out, to and from his or her bed. Some of these coverings or curtains

are exceedingly beautiful, being cut tastefully into fringes, and handsomely orna-
mented with porcupine's quills and picture writings or hieroglyphics."

"From the great number of inmates in these lodges, they are necessarily very
spacious, and the number of beds considerable. It is not uncommon to see these
lodges fifty feet in diameter inside (which is an immense room), with a row of
these curtained beds extending quite around their sides, being some ten or twelve
of them, placed four or five feet apart, and the space between them occupied by a
large post, fixed quite firm in the ground, and six or seven feet high, with large
wooden pegs or bolts on it, on which are hung and grouped, with a wild and startling taste, the arms and armour of the respective proprietor; consisting of his
whitened shield, embossed and emblazoned with the figure of his protecting medicine (or mystery), his bow and quiver, his war-club or battle-axe, his dart or javelin
– his tobacco pouch and pipe – his medicine bag – and his eagle – ermine or raven
headdress; and over all, and on the top of the post) as if placed by some conjuror
or Indian magician, to guard and protect the spell of wildness that reigns in this
strange place), stands forth and in full relief the head and horns of a buffalo,
which is, by a village regulation, owned and possessed by every man in the nation,
and hung at the head of his bed, which he uses as a mask when called upon by the
chiefs, to join in the buffalo-dance, of which I shall say more in the future epistle."

"This arrangement of beds, of arms, etc., combining the most vivid display and
arrangement of colours, of furs, of trinkets – of barbed and glistening points and
steel – of mysteries and hocus pocus, together with the sombre and smoked colour
of the roof and sides of the lodge; and the wild, and rude and red – the graceful
(though uncivil) conversational, garrulous, story telling and happy, though ignorant and untutored groups, that are smoking their pipes – wooing their sweet-
hearts, and embracing their little ones about their peaceful and endeared fire-sides;
together with their pots and kettles, spoons, and other culinary articles of their
own manufacture, around them; present altogether, one of the most picturesque
scenes to the eye of a stranger, that can be possibly seen; and far more wild and
vivid than could be imagined."

"Reader, I said these people were garrulous, story-telling and happy; this is true,
and literally so; and it belongs to me to establish the fact, and correct the error
which seems to have gone forth to the entire world on this subject. As I have before
observed, there is no subject that I know of, within the scope and reach of human

wisdom, on which the civilized world in this enlightened age are more incorrectly informed, than upon that of the true manners and customs, and moral conditions, rights and abuses, of the North American Indians; and that, as I have also before remarked, chiefly on account of the difficulty of our cultivating a fair and honourable acquaintance with them, and doing them the justice, and ourselves the credit, of a fair and impartial investigation of their true character. The present age of refinement and research has brought every thing else that I know of (and a vast deal more than the most enthusiastic mind ever dreamed of) within the scope and fair estimation of refined intellect and of science; while the wild and timid savage, with his interesting customs and modes has vanished, or his character has become changed, at the approach of the enlightened and intellectual world; who follow him like a phantom for a while, and in ignorance of his true character at last turn back to the common business and social transactions of life."

"Owing to the above difficulties, which have stood in the way, the world has fallen into many egregious errors with regard to the true modes and meaning of the savage, which I am striving to set forth and correct in the course of these epistles. And amongst them all, there is none more common, nor more entirely erroneous, nor more easily refuted, than the current one, that 'the Indian is a sour, morose, reserved and taciturn man'. I have heard this opinion advanced a thousand times and I believe it; but such certainly, is not uniformly nor generally the case."

"I have observed in all my travels amongst the Indian tribes, and more particularly amongst these unassuming people, that they are a far more talkative and conversational race than can easily be seen in the civilized world. This assertion, like many others I shall occasionally make, will somewhat startle the folks at the East, yet it is true. No one can look into the wigwams of these people, or into any little momentary group of them, without being at once struck with the conviction that small-talk, gossip, garrulity, and story-telling, are the leading passions with them, who have little else to do in the world, but to while away their lives in the innocent and endless amusement and the exercise of those talents with which Nature has liberally endowed them, for their mirth and enjoyment."

"One has but to walk or ride about this little town and its environs for a few hours and a pleasant day, and overlook the numerous games and gambols, where their notes and yelps of exultation are inceasingly vibrating in the atmosphere; or peek into their wigwams (and watch the glistening that's beaming from the noses, cheeks, and chins, of the crouching, crosslegged, and prostrate groups around the fire; where the pipe is passed, and jokes and anecdotes, and laughter are excessive) to become convinced that it is natural to laugh and be merry. Indeed it would be strange if a race of people like these, who have little else to do or relish in life, should be curtaned in that source of pleasure and amusement; and it would be also strange, if a life-time of indulgence and practice in so innocent and productive a mode of amusement, free from the cares and anxieties of business or professions, should not advance them in their modes, and enable them to draw far greater pleasure from such sources, than we in the civilized and business world can possibly feel. If the uncultivated condition of their minds curtails the number of their enjoyments; yet they are free from, and independent of, a thousand cares and jealousies, which arise from mercenary motives in the civilized world; and are yet far ahead of us (in my opinion) in the real and uninterrupted enjoyment of their simple natural faculties."

"They live in a country and in communities, where it is not customary to look forward into the future with concern, for they live without incurring the expenses of life, which are absolutely necessary and unavoidable in the enlightened world; and of course their inclinations and faculties are solely directed to the enjoyment of the present day, without the sober reflections on the past or apprehensions of the future."

"With minds thus unexpanded and uninfluenced by the thousand passions and ambitions of civilized life, it is easy and natural to concentrate their thoughts and their conversation upon the little and trying occurrences of their lives. They are fond of fun and good cheer, and can laugh easily and heartily at a slight joke, of which their peculiar modes of life furnish them an inexhaustible fund, and enable them to cheer their little circle about the wigwam fire-side with endless laughter and garrulity."

"It may be thought, that I am taking a great deal of pains to establish this fact, and I am dwelling longer upon it than I otherwise should, inasmuch as I am opposing an error that seems to have become current through the world; at which, if it be once corrected, removes a material difficulty which has always stood in the way of a fair and just estimation of the Indian character. For the purpose of placing the Indian in a proper light before the world, as I hope to do in many respects, it is of importance to me – it is but justice to the savage – and justice to my read-ers also, that such points should be cleared up as I proceed; and for the world who enquire for correct and just information, they must take my words for the truth, or else come to this country and look for themselves, into these grotesque circles of never ending laughter and fun, instead of going to Washington City to gaze on the poor embarrassed Indian who is called there by his 'Great Father', to contend with the sophistry of the learned and acquisitive world, in bartering away his lands with the graves and the hunting grounds of his ancestors. There is not the proper place to study the Indian character; yet it is the place where the sycophant and the scrib-bler go to gaze and frown upon him – to learn his character, and write his histo-ry! And because he does not speak, and quaffs the delicious beverage which he receives from white mens' hands, 'he's a speechless brute and a drunkard'. An Indian is a beggar in Washington City, and a white man is almost equally so in the Mandan village. An Indian in Washington is mute, is dumb and embarrassed; and so is a white man (and for the very same reasons) in this place – he has nobody to talk to."

"A wild Indian, to reach the civilized world, must needs travel some thousands of miles in vehicles of conveyance, to which he is unaccustomed – through lati-tudes and longitudes which are new to him – living on food that he is unused to – stared and gazed at by the thousands and tens of thousands whom he cannot talk to – his heart grieving and his body sickening at the exhibition of white men's wealth and luxuries, which are enjoyed on the land, and over the bones of his ancestors. And at the end of his journey he stands (like a caged animal) to be scanned – to be criticized – to be pitied – and heralded to the world as a mute – as a brute, and a beggar."

"A white man, to reach this village, must travel by steam-boat – by canoes – on horseback and on foot; swim rivers – wade quagmires – fight mosquitoes – patch his moccasins, and patch them again and again, and his breeches; live on meat alone – sleep on the ground the whole way, and think and dream of his friends he has left behind; and when he gets there, half-starved, and half- naked, and more than half sick, he finds himself a beggar for a place to sleep, and for something to eat; a mute amongst thousands who flock about him, to look and to criticize, and to laugh at him for his jaded appearance, and to speak of him as they do of all white men (without distinction) as liars. These people are in the habit of seeing no white men in their country but Traders, and know of no other deeming us all alike, and receiving us all under the presumption that we come to trade or barter; applying to us all, indiscriminately, the epithet of "liars" or Traders."

"The reader will therefore see, that we mutually suffer in each other's estimation from the unfortunate ignorance, which distance has chained us in; and (as I can vouch, and the Indian also, who has visited the civilized world) that the historian who would record justly and correctly the character and customs of a people, must go and live among them."

George Catlin's painting of Mandan bull boats with a Mandan village in the background.
Photo courtesy of the Minnesota Historical Society

LETTER NO. 13 FROM GEORGE CATLIN'S BOOK, "LETTERS AND NOTES ON THE MANNERS, CUSTOMS, AND CONDITIONS OF THE NORTH AMERICAN INDIANS" (FIRST PUBLISHED IN LONDON, ENGLAND, IN 1844)

MANDAN VILLAGE, UPPER MISSOURI

"In several of my former letters I have given sketches of the village, and some few of the customs of these peculiar people; and I have many more yet in store; some of which will induce the readers to laugh, and others almost dispose them to weep. But at present, I drop them, and introduce a few of the wild and gentle-manly Mandans themselves; and first, Ha-natah-nu-mauh, the wolf chief. This man is head-chief of the nation, and familiarly known by the name of "Chef de Loup", as the French Traders call him; a haughty, austere, and overbearing man, respect-ed and feared by his people rather than loved. The tenure by which this man holds his office, is that by which the head-chiefs of most of the tribes claim, that of inher-itance. It is a general, though not an infallible rule amongst the numerous tribes of North American Indians, that the office of chief belongs to the eldest son of a chief, provided he shows himself, by his conduct, to be equally worthy of it as any other in the nation; making it hereditary on a very proper condition – in default of which requisites, or others which may happen, the office is elective."

"The dress of this chief was one of great extravagance, and some beauty; manufactured of skins, and a great number of quills of the raven, forming his stylish head-dress."

"The next and second chief of the tribe, is Mah-to-toh-pa (the four bears). This extraordinary man, through second in office is undoubtedly the first and most popular man in the nation. Free, generous, elegant and gentlemanly in his deportment – handsome, brave and valiant; wearing a robe on his back, with the history of his battles emblazoned on it; which would fill a book of themselves, if properly translated. This, readers, is the most extraordinary man, perhaps, who lives at this day, in the atmosphere of Nature's noblemen; and I shall certainly tell you more of him anon."

"After him, there are Mah-tahp-ta-ha, he who rushes through the middle; Seehk-hee-da, the mouse-coloured feather; Sanja-ka-ko-kah (the deceiving wolf); Mah-to-he-ha (the old bear), and others, distinguished as chiefs and warriors – and there are others also; such as Mi-neek-e-sunk-te-ca, the mink; and the little grayhaired Sha-ko-kn, and fifty others, who are famous for their conquests, not with the bow or the javelin, but with their small black eyes, which shoot out from under their unfledged brows, and pierce the oldest, fiercest chieftain to the heart."

"The Mandans are certainly a very interesting and pleasing people in their personal appearance and manners; differing in many respects, both in looks and customs, from all other tribes which I have seen. They are not a warlike people; for they seldom, if ever, carry war into their enemies' country; but when invaded, show their valour and courage to be equal to that of any people on earth. Being a small tribe, and unable to contend on the wide prairies with the Sioux and other roaming tribes, which are ten times more numerous; they have very judiciously located themselves in a permanent village, which is strongly fortified, and ensures their preservation. By this means they have advanced further in the arts of manufacture; have supplied their lodges more abundantly with the comforts, and even luxuries of life, than any Indian nation I know of. The consequence of this is, that this tribe has taken many steps ahead of other tribes in manners and refinements (if I may be allowed to apply the word refinement to Indian life); and are therefore familiarly (and correctly) denominated, by the Traders and others, who have been amongst them, "the polite and friendly Mandans"."

"There is certainly great justice in the remark; and so forcibly have I been struck with the peculiar ease and elegance of these people, together with the diversity of complexions, the various colours of their hair and eyes; the singularity of their language, and their peculiar and unaccountable customs, that I am fully convinced that they have sprung from some other origin than that of the other North American tribes, or that they are an amalgam of natives with some civilized race. Here arises a question of very great interest and importance for discussion; and, after further familiarity with their character, customs, and traditions, if I forget it not, I will eventually give it further consideration. Suffice it then, for the present, that their personal appearance alone, independant of their modes and customs, pronounces them at once, as more or less, than savage."

"A stranger in the Mandan village is first struck with the different shades of complexion, and various colours of hair which he sees in a crowd about him; and is at once almost disposed to exclaim that "these are not Indian"."

I interrupt Catlin's monologue at this point to focus your attention on what he is reporting: These are no ordinary Indians. His observations aren't casual, but studies; not off-hand, but catalogued. He believes he's announcing an important discovery, one of the most important of this entire series of letters.

"There are a great many of these people whose complexions appear as light as half breeds; and amongst the women particularly, there are many whose skins are almost white, with the most pleasing symmetry and proportion of features; with hazel, with grey, and with blue eyes, – with mildness and sweetness of expression, and excessive modesty of demeanour, which render them exceedingly pleasing and beautiful."

"Why this diversity of complexion I cannot tell, nor can they themselves account for it. their traditions, so far as I have yet learned them, afford us no information of their having had any knowledge of white men before the visit of Lewis and Clarke[1], made to their village thirty-three years ago. Since that time there have been but very few visits from white men to this place, and surely not enough to

---

[1] Apparently no mention was made of the La Verendryes, but that is not surprising since their visit was nearly 100 years earlier.

have changed the complexions and the customs of a nation. And I recollect perfectly well that Governor Clarke told me, before I started for this place, that I would find the Mandans a strange people and half white."

"The diversity in the colour of hair is also equally as great as that in the complexion; for in a numerous group of these people (and more particularly amongst the females, who never take pains to change its natural colour, as the men often do), there may be seen every shade and colour of hair that can be seen in our own country, with the exception of red or auburn, which is not to be found."

"This singular and eccentric appearance is much oftener seen among the women than it is with the men; for many of the latter who have it, seem ashamed of it, and artfully conceal it, by filling their hair with glue and black and red earth. The women, on the other hand, seem proud of it, and display it often in an almost incredible profusion, which spreads over their shoulders and falls as low as the knee. I have ascertained, on a careful inquiry, that about one in ten or twelve of the whole tribe are what the French call "cheveux gris", or greyhairs; and that is strange and un-accountable phenomenon is not the result of disease or habit; but that it is unquestionably a hereditary character which runs in families, and indicates no inequality in disposition or intellect. And by passing this hair through my hands, as I often have, I have found it uniformly to be as coarse and harsh as a horse's mane; differing materially from the hair of other colours, which amongst the Mandans, is generally as fine and as soft as silk."

"The reader will at once see, by the above facts, that there is enough upon the faces and heads of these people to stamp them peculiar, – when he meets them in the heart of this almost boundless wilderness, presenting such diversities of colour in the complexion and hair; when he knows from what he as seen, and what he has read, that all other primitive tribes known in America, are dark copper-coloured, with jet black hair."

"From these few facts alone, the reader will see that I am amongst a strange and interesting people, and know how to pardon me, if I lead him through a maze of novelty and mysteries to the knowledge of a strange, yet kind and hospitable, people, whose fate, like that of all their race is sealed; – and unaccountable peculiar, which on earth; nor on any rational grounds whose doom is fixed, to live just long enough to be imperfectly known, and then to fall before the disease or sword of civilizing devastation."

"The stature of the Mandans is rather below the ordinary size of man[1], with beauty of form and proportion, and wonderful suppleness and elasticity; they are pleasingly erect and graceful, both in their walk and their attitudes; and the hair of the men, which generally spreads over their backs, falling down to the hams, and sometimes to the ground, is divided into Plaits or slabs of two inches in width, and filled with a profusion of glue and red earth or vermillion, at intervals of an inch or two, which becoming very hard, remains in and unchanged from year to year."

"This mode of dressing the hair is curious, and gives to the Mandans the most singular appearance. The hair of the men is uniformly all laid over from the forehead backwards; carefully kept above and resting on the ear, and thence falling down over the back, in these flattened bunches, and painted red, extending oftimes quite on to the calf of the leg, and some times in such profusion as almost to conceal the whole figure from the person walking behind them. In the portrait of San-ja-ka-ko-kall (the deceiving wolf), where he is represented at full length, with several others of His family around him in a group, there will be seen a fair illustration of these and other customs of these people."

"The hair of the women is also worn as long as they can possibly cultivate it, oiled very often, which preserves on it a beautiful gloss and shows its natural colour. They often braid it in two large plaits, one falling down just back of the ear, on each side of the head; and on any occasion which requires them to "put on their best looks", they pass their fingers through it, drawing it out of braid, and spreading it over their shoulders. The Mandan women observe strictly the same custom, which I observed amongst the Crows and Blackfeet (and, in fact, all other tribes I have seen, without a single exception), of parting the hair on the forehead, and always keeping the crease or separation filled with vermilion or other red paint. this is one of the very few little (and apparently trivial) customs which I have found amongst the Indians, without being able to assign any cause for it, other than that "they are Indians", and that this is an Indian fashion."

"In mourning, like the Crows and most other tribes, the women are obliged to crop their hair all off; and the usual term of that condolence is until the hair has grown again to its former length."

---

[1] Interesting because La Verendrye characterized the Mandans as taller than average. Is it possible that these taller, larger people were more vulnerable to disease and that their genes were lost?

"When a man mourns for the death of a near relation the case is quite different; his long, valued tresses, are of much greater importance and only a lock or two can be spared. Just enough to tell of his grief to his friends, without destroying his most valued ornament, in doing just reverence and respect to the dead."

"To repeat what I have said before, the Mandans are a pleasing and friendly race of people, of whom it is proverbial amongst the Traders and all who ever have know them, that their treatment of white men in their country has been friendly and kind ever since their first acquaintance with them – they have ever met and received them, on the prairie or in their villages, with hospitality and honour."

"They are handsome, straight and elegant in their forms – not tall, but quick and graceful; easy and polite in their manners, neat in their persons and beautifully clad. When I say "neat in person and beautifully clad", however, I do not intend my readers to understand that such is the case with them all, for among them and most other tribes, as with the enlightened world, there are different grades of society – those who care but little for their personal appearance, and those who take great pains to please themselves and their friends. Amongst this class of personages, such as chiefs and braves, or warriors of distinction, and their families, and dandies or exquisites (a class of beings of whom I shall take due time to speak in a future letter), the strictest regard to decency, and cleanliness and elegance of dress is observed; and there are few people, perhaps, who take more pains to keep their persons neat and clean than they do."

"At the distance of half a mile or so above the village, is the customary place where the women and girls resort every morning in the summer months, to bathe in the river. To this spot they repair by hundreds, every morning at sunrise, where, on a beautiful beach, they can be seen running and glistening in the sun, whilst they are playing their innocent gambols and leaping into the stream. They all learn to swim well, and the poorest swimmer amongst them will dash fearlessly into the boiling, and eddying current of the Missouri, and cross it with perfect ease. At the distance of a quarter of a mile back from the river, extends a terrace or elevated prairie, running north from the village, and forming a kind of semicircle around this bathing place; and on this terrace, which is some twenty or thirty feet higher than the meadow between it and the river, are stationed every morning several sentinels, with their bows and arrows in hand, to guard and protect this sacred ground from the approach of boys or men from any direction."

"At a little distance below the village, also, is the place where the men and boys go to bathe and learn to swim. After this morning ablution, they return to their village, wipe their limbs dry, and use a profusion of bear's grease through their hair and over their bodies."

"The art of swimming is known to all the American Indians; and perhaps no people in earth have taken more pains to learn it, nor any who turn it to better account. There certainly are no people whose avocations of life more often call for the use of their limbs in this way; as many of the tribes spend their lives on the shores of our vast lakes and rivers, paddling about in their childhood in their fragile bark canoes, which are liable to continual accidents, which often throw the Indian upon his natural resources for the preservation of his life."

"There are many times also, when out upon their long marches in the prosecution of their almost continued warfare, when it becomes necessary to plunge into and swim across the wildest streams and rivers, at times when they have no canoes or draft in which to cross them. I have as yet seen no tribe where this art is neglected. It is learned at a very early age by both sexes, and enables the strong and hardy muscles of the squaws to take their child upon the back and successfully to pass any river that lies in their way."

"The mode of swimming amongst the Mandans, as well as amongst most of the other tribes, is quite different from that practiced in those parts of the civilized world, which I have had the pleasure yet to visit. The Indian, instead of parting his hands simultaneously under the chin, and making the stroke outward, in a horizontal direction, causing thereby a serious strain upon the chest, throws his body alternately upon the left to the right side, raising one arm entirely above the water and reaching as far forward as he can, to dip it, whilst his whole weight and force are spent upon the one that is passing under him, and like a paddle propelling him along; whilst this arm is making a half circle, and is being raised out of the water behind him, the opposite arm is describing a similar arch in the air over his head, to be dipped in the water as far as he can reach before him, with the hand turned under, forming a sort of bucket, to act most effectively as it passes in its turn underneath him."

"By this bold and powerful mode of swimming, which may want the grace that many would wish to see, I am quite sure, from the experience I have had, that much of the fatigue and strain upon the breast and spine are avoided, and that a man will preserve his strength and his breath much longer in this alternate and rolling motion, than he can in the usual mode of swimming, in the polished world."

"In addition to the modes of bathing which I have above described, the Mandans have another, which is a much greater luxury, and often resorted to by the sick, but far more often by the well and sound, as a matter of luxury only, or perhaps for the purpose of hardening their limbs and preparing them for the thousand exposures and vicissitudes of life to which they are continually liable. I allude to their vapour baths, or sudatories, of which each village has several, and which seem to be a kind of public property accessible to all, and resorted to by all, male and female, old and young, sick and well."

"In every Mandan lodge is to be seen a crib or basket, much in the shape of a bathing-tub, curiously woven with willow boughs, and sufficiently large to receive any person of the family in a reclining or recumbent posture; which, when any one is to take a bath, is carried by the squaw to the sudatory for that purpose, and brought back to the wigwam again after it has been used."

"These sudatories are always near the village, above or below it, on the bank of the river. They are generally built of skins (in form of a Crow or Sioux lodge which I have before described), covered with buffalo skins sewed tight together, with a kind of furnace in the centre; or in other words, in the centre of the lodge are two walls of stone about six feet long and two and a half apart, and about three feet high; across and over this space, between the two walls, are laid a number of round sticks, on which the bathing crib is placed. Contiguous to the lodge, and outside of it, is a little furnace or something similar, in the side of the bank, where the woman kindles a hot fire, and heats to a red heat a number of large stones, which are kept at these places for this particular purpose; and having them all in readiness, she goes home or sends word to inform her husband or other one who is waiting, that all is ready; when he makes his appearance entirely naked, though with a large buffalo robe wrapped around him. He then enters the lodge and places himself in the crib or basket, either on his back or in a sitting posture (the latter of which is generally preferred), with his back towards the door of the lodge; when the squaw brings in a large stone red hot, between two sticks (lashed together somewhat in the form of a pair of tongs) and, placing it under him, throws cold water upon it, which raises a profusion of vapour about him. He is at once enveloped in a cloud of steam, and a woman or child will sit at a little distance and continue to dash water upon the stone, whilst the matron of the lodge is out, and preparing to make her appearance with another heated stone: or he will sit and dip from a wooden bowl, with a ladle made of the mountain-sheep's horn, and throw upon the heated stones, with his own hands, the water which he is drawing through his lungs and pores, in the next moment, in the most delectable and exhilarating vapours, as it distills through the mat of wild sage and other medicinal and aromatic herbs, which he has strewed over the bottom of his basket, and on which he reclines."

"During all this time the lodge is shut perfectly tight, and he quaffs this delicious and renovating draught to his lungs with deep drawn sighs, and with extended nostrils, until he is drenched in the most profuse degree of perspiration that can be produced; when he makes a kind of strangled signal, at which the lodge is opened, and he darts forth with the speed of a frightened deer, and plunges headlong into the river, from which he instantly escapes again, wraps his robe around him and "leans" as fast as possible for home. Here his limbs are wiped dry, and wrapped close and tight within the fur of the buffalo robes, in which he takes his nap, with his feet to the fire; then oils his limbs and hair with bear's grease, dresses and plumes himself for a visit – a feast – a parade, or a council; or slicks down his long hair, and rubs his oiled limbs to a polish, with a piece of soft buckskin, prepared to join in games of ball or chung-kee."

"Such is the sudatory or the vapour bath of the Mandans, and, as I before observed, it is resorted to both as an everyday luxury by those who have the time and energy or industry to indulge in it; and also used by the sick as a remedy for nearly all the diseases which are know amongst them.

"Fevers are very rare, and in fact almost unknown amongst these people: but in the few cases of fever which have been known, this treatment has been applied, and without the fatal consequences which we would naturally predict. The greater part of their diseases are inflammatory rheumatisms, and other chronic diseases; and for these, this mode of treatment, with their modes of life, does admirably well. this custom is similar amongst nearly all of these Missouri Indians, and amongst the Pawnees, Omahas, and Punchas and other tribes, which have suffered with the smallpox (the dread destroyer of the Indian race), this mode was practiced by the poor creatures, who fled by hundreds to the river's edge, and by hundreds died before they could escape from the waves, into which they had plunged in the heat and rage of a burning fever. Such will yet be the scourge, and such the misery of these poor unthinking people, and each tribe to the Rocky Mountains, as it has been with every tribe between here and the Atlantic Ocean. White man's whiskey – tomahawks – scalping knives – guns, powder and ball – smallpox – debaucher – extermination."

1838 — THE DEMISE OF THE MANDANS

Who better than George Catlin to describe the extermination of these people he loved so much? We shall quote directly from his book.

"From the accounts brought to New York in the fall of 1838, by Messrs. McKenzie, Mitchell, and others, from the Upper Missouri, and with whom I conversed on the subject, it seems that in the summer of that year the small-pox was accidentally introduced amongst the Mandans, by the Fur Traders; and that in the course of two months they all perished, except some thirty or forty, who were taken as slaves by the Riccarees; an enemy living two hundred miles below them, and who moved up and took possession of their village soon after their calamity, taking up their residence in it, it being a better built village than their own; and from the lips of one of the traders who had more recently arrived from there, I had the following account of the remaining few, in whose destruction was the final termination of this interesting and once numerous tribe."

"The Riccarees, he said, had taken possession of the village after the disease had subsided, and after living some months in it, were attacked by a large party of their enemies, the Sioux, and whilst fighting desperately in resistance, in which the Mandan prisoners had taken an active part, the latter had concerted a plan for their own destruction, which was effected by their simultaneously running through the piquets on to the prairie, calling out to the Sioux (both men and women) to kill them, "that they were Riccaree dogs, that their friends were all dead, and they did not wish to live," – that they here wielded their weapons as desperately as they could, to excite the fury of their enemy, and that they were thus cut to pieces and destroyed."

"The accounts given by two or three white men, who were amongst the Mandans during the ravages of this rightful disease, are most appalling and actually too heart-rendering and disgusting to be recorded. The disease was introduced in the country by the Fur Company's steamer from St. Louis; which had two of their crew sick with the disease when it approached the Upper Missouri, and imprudently stopped to trade at the Mandan village, which was on the bank of the river, where the chiefs and other were allowed to come on board, by which means the disease got ashore."

"I am constrained to believe, that the gentlemen in charge of the steamer did not believe it to be the small-pox; for if they had know it to be such, I cannot conceive of such imprudence, as regarded their own interests in the country, as well as the fate of these poor people, by allowing their boat to advance into the country under such circumstances."

"It seems that the Mandans were surrounded by several war-parties of their more powerful enemies the Sioux, at that unlucky time, and they could not therefore disperse upon the plains, by which many of them could have been saved; and they were necessarily inclosed within the piquets of their village, where the disease in a few days became so very malignant that death ensued in a few hours after its attacks; and so slight were their hopes when they were attacked, that nearly half of them destroyed themselves with their knives, with their guns, and by dashing their brains out by leaping head-foremost from a thirty food ledge of rocks in front of their village. The first symptom of the disease was a rapid swelling of the body, and so very virulent had it become, that very many died in two or three hours after their attack, and that in many cases without the appearance of the disease upon the skin. Utter dismay seemed to possess all classes and all ages, and they gave themselves up in despair, as entirely lost. There was but one continual crying and howling and praying to the Great Spirit for his protection during the nights and days; and there being but few living, and those in too appalling despair, nobody thought of burying the dead, whose bodies, whole families together, were left in horrid and loathsome piles in their own wigwams, with a few buffalo robes thrown over them, there to decay, and be devoured by their own dogs. That such a proportion of their community as that above-mentioned, should have perished in so short a time, seems yet to the reader, an unaccountable thing; but in addition to the causes just mentioned, it must be borne in mind that this frightful disease is everywhere far more fatal amongst the native than in civilized population, which may be owing to some extraordinary constitutional susceptibility; or, I think, more probably, to the exposed lives they live, leading more directly to fatal consequences. In this, as in most of their diseases, they ignorantly and imprudently plunge into the coldest water, whilst in the highest state of fever, and often die before they have the power to get out."

"Some have attributed the unexampled fatality of this disease amongst the Indians to the fact of their living entirely on animal food; but so important a subject for investigation I must leave for sounder judgments than mine to decide. They are a people whose constitutions and habits of life enable them most certainly to meet most of its ills with less dread, and with decidedly greater success, than they are met in civilized communities; and I would not dare to decide that their simple meat diet was the cause of their fatal exposure to one frightful disease, when I am decidedly of opinion that it has been the cause of their exemption and protection from another, almost equally destructive, and, like the former, of civilized introduction."

"During the season of the ravages of the Asiatic cholera which swept over the greater parts of the western country, and the Indian frontier, I was a traveller through those regions, and was able to witness its effects; and I learned from what I saw, as well as from what I have heard in other parts since that time, that it travelled to and over the frontiers, carrying dismay and death amongst the tribes on the borders in many cases, so far as they had adopted the civilized modes of life, with its dissipations, using vegetable food and salt; but wherever it came to the tribes living exclusively on meat, and that without the use of salt, its progress was suddenly stopped. I mention this as a subject which I looked upon as important to science, and therefore one on which I made many careful enquires; and so far as I have learned along that part of the frontier over which I have since passed, I have to my satisfaction ascertained that such became the utmost limits of this fatal disease in its travel to the West, unless where it might have followed some of the routes of the Fur Traders, who, of course, have introduced the modes of civilized life."

"From the Trader who was present at the destruction of the Mandans I had many most wonderful incidents of this dreadful scene, but I dread to recite them. Amongst them, however, there is one that I must briefly describe, relative to the death of that noble gentleman of whom I have already said so much, and to whom I became so much attached, Mah-to-toh-pa, or "The Four Beard". This fine fellow sat in his wigwam and watched everyone of his family die about him, his wives and his little children, after he had recovered from the disease himself; when he walked out, around the village, and wept over the final destruction of his tribe; his braves and warriors, whose sinewy arms alone he could depend on for a continuance of their existence, all laid low; when he came back to his lodge, where he covered his whole family in a pile, with a number of robes, and wrapping another around himself, went out upon a hill at a little distance where he laid several days, despite all the solicitations of the Traders, resolved to starve himself to death. He remained there till the sixth day, when he had just strength enough to creep back to the village, when he entered the horrid gloom of his own wigwam, and laying his body along-side of the group of his family, drew his rob over him and died on the ninth day of his fatal abstinence."

"So have perished the friendly and hospitable Mandans, from the best accounts I could get; and although it may be possible that some few individuals may yet be remaining, I think it is not probable; and one thing is certain, even if such be the case, that, as a nation, the Mandans are extinct, having no longer an existence."

"There is yet a melancholy part of the tale to be told, relating to the ravages of this frightful disease in that country on the same occasion, as it spread to other contiguous tribes, to the Minatarres, the Knisteneaux, the Blackfeet, the Chayennes and Crows; amongst whom 25,000 perished in the course of four or five months, which most appalling facts I got from Major Pilcher, now Superintendent of Indian Affairs at St. Louis, from Mr. McKenzie, and others."

"It may be naturally asked here, by the reader, whether the Government of the United States have taken any measures to prevent the ravages of this fatal disease amongst these exposed tribes; to which I answer, that repeated efforts have been made, and so far generally, as the tribes have ever had the disease, (or, at all events, within the recollections of those who are now living in the tribes,) the Government agents have succeeded in introducing vaccination as a protection; but amongst those tribes in their wild state, and where they have not suffered with the disease, very little success has been met with in the attempt to protect them, on account of their superstitions, which have generally resisted all attempts to introduce vaccination. Whilst I was on the Upper Missouri, several surgeons were sent into the country with the Indian agents, where I several times saw the attempts made without success. They have perfect confidence in the skill of their own physicians, until the disease has made one slaughter in their tribe, and then, having seen white man amongst them protected by it, they are disposed to receive it, before which they cannot believe that so minute a puncture in the arm is going to protect them from so fatal a disease; and as they see white men so earnestly urging it, they decide that it must be some new mode or trick of pale faces, by which they are to gain some new advantage over them, and they stubbornly and successfully resist it."

CHAPTER TWO

THE WELSH CONNECTION

Many authors before Catlin told the story of Prince Madoc's ten ships that left Wales in 1170 and never returned. These writers as well as several who followed Catlin told slightly different stories but we have chosen Catlin to tell it first in this book because the readers are now accustomed to his style and because, in our estimation, he does the best job of connecting the Welsh excursion to the Mandans. Other abbreviated versions will follow.

THE WELSH COLONY
BY GEORGE CATLIN

"Which I barely spoke of in page 206, of Vol. I. which sailed under the direction of Prince Madoc, or Madawc, from North Wales, in the early part of the fourteenth century in ten ships, according to numerous and accredited authors, and never returned to their own country, have been supposed to have landed somewhere on the coast of North or South America; and from the best authorities, (which I will suppose everybody has read, rather than quote them at this time), I believe it has been pretty clear proved that they landed either on the coast of Florida, or about the mouth of the Mississippi, and according to the history and poetry of their country, settled somewhere in the interior of North America, where they are yet remaining, intermixed with some of the savage tribes."

"In my letter just referred to, I barely suggested, that the Mandans, whom I found with so many peculiarities in looks and customs, which I have already described, might possibly be the remains of this lost colony, amalgamated with a tribe, or part of a tribe, of the natives, which would account for the unusual appearances of this tribe of Indians, and also for the changed character and customs of the Welsh Colonists, provided these be the remains of them."

"Since those notes were written, as will have been seen by my subsequent letters, and particularly in page 9 of this Volume, I have descended the Missouri River from the Mandan village to St. Louis, a distance of 180 miles, and have taken pains to examine its shores; and from the repeated remains of the ancient locations of the Mandans, which I met with on the banks of that river, I am fully convinced that I have traced them down nearly to the mouth of the Ohio River; and from exactly similar appearances, which I recollect to have seen several years since in several places in the interior of the state of Ohio, I am fully convinced that they have formerly occupied that part of the country, and have, from some cause or other, been put in motion, and continued to make their repeated moves until they arrived at the place of their residence at the time of their extinction, on the Upper Missouri."

"In the annexed chart of the Missouri and Ohio rivers, will be seen laid down the different positions of the ancient marks of their towns which I have examined; and also, nearly, (though not exactly) the positions of the very numerous civilized fortifications which are now remaining on the Ohio and Muskingum rivers, in the vicinity of which I believe the Mandans once lived."

"These ancient fortifications, which are very numerous in that vicinity, some of which enclose a great many acres, and being built on the banks of the rivers, with walls in some places twenty or thirty feet in height, with covered ways to the water, evidence a knowledge of the science of fortifications, apparently not a century behind that of the present day, were evidently never built by any nation of savages in America, and present to us incontestable proof of the former existence of a people very far advanced in the arts of civilization, who have, from some cause or other, disappeared, and left these imperishable proofs of their former existence."

"Now I am inclined to believe that the ten ships of Madoc, or a part of them at least, entered the Mississippi river at the Balize, and made their way up the Mississippi, or that they landed somewhere on the Florida coast, and that their brave and preserving colonists made their way through the interior, to a position on the Ohio river, where they cultivated their fields, and established in one of the finest countries on earth, a flourishing colony; but were at length set upon by the savages, whom, perhaps, they provoked to warfare, being trespassers on their hunting-grounds, and by whom, in overpowering hordes, they were besieged, until it was necessary to erect these fortifications for their defense, into which they were at last driven by a confederacy of tribes, and their held till their ammunition and provisions gave out, and they in the end have all perished, except, perhaps, that portion of them who might have formed alliance by marriage with the Indians, and their offspring, who would have been half-breeds, and of course attached to the Indians' side; whose lives have been spared in the general massacre; and at length, being despised, as all half-breeds of enemies are, have gathered themselves into a band, and severing from their parent tribe, have moved off, and increased in numbers and strength, as they have advanced up the Missouri river to the place where they have been known for many years past by the name of the Mandans, a corruption of abbreviation, perhaps, of "Madawgwys", the name applied by the Welsh to the followers of Madawc."

"If this be a startling theory for the world, they will be the more sure to read the following brief reasons which I bring in support of my opinion; and if they do not support me, they will at least be worth knowing, and may, at the same time, be the means of eliciting further and more successful enquiry."

"As I have said, in page 9 of this Volume, and in other places, the marks of the Mandan villages are known by the excavations of two feet or more in depth, and thirty or forty feet in diameter, of a circular form, made in the ground for the foundations of their wigwams, which leave a decided remains for centuries, and one that is easily detected the moment that it is met with. After leaving the Mandan village, I found the marks of their former residence about sixty miles below where they were then living, and from which they removed (from their own account) about sixty or eighty years since; and from the appearance of the number of their lodges, I should think, that at that recent date there must have been three times the number that were living when I was amongst them. Near the mouth of the big Shienne river, 200 miles below their last location, I found still more ancient remains, and in as many as six or seven other places between that and the mouth of the Ohio, as I have designated on the chart, and each one, is I visited them, appearing more and more ancient, convincing me that these people, wherever they might have come from, have gradually made their moves up the banks of the Missouri, to the place where I visited them."

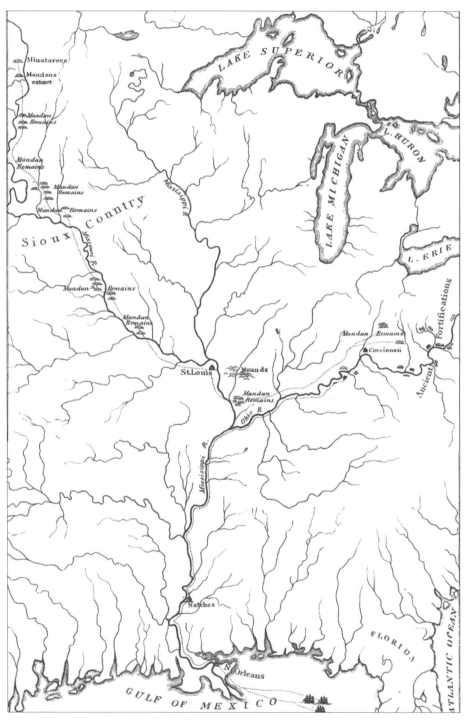

Catlin's chart showing the moves of the Mandans and the places of their extinction.

"For the most part of this distance they have been in the heart of the great Sioux country, and being looked upon by the Sioux as trespassers, have been continually warred upon by this numerous tribe, who have endeavoured to extinguish them, as they have been endeavouring to do ever since our first acquiantance with them; but who, being always fortified by a strong piquet, or stockade, have successfully withstood the assaults of their enemies, and preserved the remnant of their tribe. Through this sort of gauntlet they have run, in passing through the countries of these warlike and hostile tribes."

"It may be objected to this, perhaps, that the Riccarees and Minatarees are Crows, from the north-west; and by their own showing, fled to the Mandans for protection, and forming their villages by the side of them, built their wigwams in the same manner."

"The riccarees have been a very small tribe, far inferior to the Mandans; and by the traditions of the Mandans, as well as from the evidence of the first explorers, Lewis and Clarke, and others, have lived, until quite lately, on terms of intimacy with the Mandans, whose villages they have successively occupied as the Mandans have moved and vacated them, as they now are doing, since disease has swept the whole of the Mandans away."

"Whether my derivation of the word Mandan from Madawgwys be correct or not, I will pass over the word at present merely as presumptive proof, for want of better, which, perhaps, this enquiry may elicit; and, at the same time, I offer the Welsh word Mandon, (the woodroof, a species of madder used as a red dye), as the name that might possibly have been applied by their Welsh neighbours to these people, on account of their very ingenious mode of giving the beautiful red and other dyes to the porcupine quills with which they garnish their dresses."

"In their own language they called themselves See-pons-ka-nu-man-ka-kee, (the people of the pheasants,) which was probably the name of the primitive stock, before they were mixed with any other people; and to have got such a name, it is natural to suppose that they must have come from a country where pheasants existed, which cannot be found short of reaching the timbered country at the base of the Rocky Mountains, some six or eight hundred miles West of the Mandans, or the forests of Indiana and Ohio, some hundreds of miles to the South and East of where they last lived."

"The above facts, together with the other one which they repeatedly related to me, and which I have before alluded to, that they have often been to the hill of the Red

Pipe Stone, and that they once lived near it, carry conclusive evidence, I think, that they have formerly occupied a country much farther to the South; and that they have repeatedly changed their locations, until they reached the spot of their last residence, where they have met with their final misfortune. And as evidence in support of my opinion that they came from the banks of the Ohio, and have brought with them some of the customs of the civilized people who erected those ancient fortifications, I am able to say, that the numerous specimens of pottery which have been taken from the graves and tumuli about those ancient works, (many of which may be seen now, in the Cincinnati Museum, and some of which, my own donations, and which have so much surprised the enquiring world,) were to be seen in great numbers in the use of the Mandans; and scarcely a day in the summer, when the visitor to their village would not see the women at work with their hands and fingers, moulding them from black clay, into vases, cups, pitchers, and pots, and baking them in their little kilns in the sides of the hill, or under the bank of the river."

"In addition to this art, which I am sure belongs to no other tribe on the Continent, these people have also, as a secret with themselves, the extraordinary art of manufacturing a very beautiful and lasting kind of blue glass beads, which they wear on their necks in great quantities, and decidedly value above all others that are brought amongst them by the Fur Traders."

These are Welch bullboats on display in Wales. Inset: Mandan bullboats.
Photo couresy of the Minnesota Historical Society

"This secret is not only one that the Traders did not introduce amongst them, but one that they cannot learn from them; and at the same time, beyond a doubt, an art that has been introduced amongst them by some civilized people, as it is as yet unknown to other Indian tribes in that vicinity, or elsewhere. Of this interesting fact, Lewis and Clarke have given an account thirty-three years ago, at a time when no Traders, or other white people, had been amongst the Mandans, to have taught them so curious an art."

"The Mandan canoes which are altogether different from those of all other tribes, are exactly the Welsh coracle, made of raw-hides, the skins of buffaloes, stretched underneath a frame made of willow or other boughs, and shaped nearly round, like a tub; which the woman caries on her head from her wigwam to the water's edge, and having stepped into it, stands in front, and propels it by dipping her paddle forward, and drawing it to her, instead of paddling by the side. In referring to Plate 240, letter c, page 138, the reader will see several drawings of these seemingly awkward crafts, which nevertheless, the Mandan women will pull through the water at a rapid rate."

"How far these extraordinary facts may go in the estimation of the reader, with numerous other which I have mentioned in Volume 1, whilst speaking of the Mandans, of their various complexions, colours of hair, and blue and grey eyes, towards establishing my opinion as a sound theory, I cannot say; but this much I can safely aver, that at the moment that I first saw these people, I was so struck with the peculiarity of their appearance, that I was under the instant conviction that they were an amalgam of a native, with some civilized race; and from what I have seen of them, and of the remains on the Missouri and Ohio rivers, I feel fully convinced that these people have emigrated from the later stream; and that they have, in the manner that I have already stated, with many of their customs, been preserved from the almost total destruction of the bold colonists of Madawc, who I believe, steeled upon the occupied for a century or so, the rich and fertile banks of the Ohio. In adducing the proof for the support of this theory, if I have failed to complete it, I have the satisfaction that I have not taken up much of the reader's time, and I can therefore claim his attention a few moments longer, whilst I refer him to a brief vocabulary of the Mandan language in the following pages, where he may compare it with that of the Welsh; and better, perhaps, than I can, decide whether there is any affinity existing between the two; and if he finds it, it will bring me a friendly aid in support of the position I have taken."

"From the comparison, that I have been able to make, I think I am authorized to say, that the following list of words, which form a part of that vocabulary, there is a striking similarity, and quite sufficient to excite surprise in the minds of the attentive reader, if it could be proved that those resemblances were but the results of accident between two foreign and distinct idioms."

English	Mandan	Welsh	Pronounced
I	Me	Mi	Me
You	Ne	Chwi	Chwe
He	E	A	A
She	Ea	E	A
It	Ount	Hwynt	Hooynt
We	Noo	Ni	Ne
They	Eonah	Hwna *MAS.*	Hoona
		Hona *FEM.*	Hona
Those ones		Yrhai Hyna	
No, or, There is not	Megosh	Nagoes	Nagosh
No		Nage	
		Nag	
		Na	
Head	Pan	Pen	Pan
The Great Spirit	Maho peneta	Mawr Penaethir [*]	Maoor Panaether
		Ysprid mawr [†]	

[*] To act as a great chief, head or principal, sovereign or supreme
[†] The Great Spirit

Catlin talks about the secret process the Mandans had of manufacturing bright blue beads for use in all kinds of decorations. It is probably no coincidence that the same beads were manufactured in Wales.

SO JUST WHO WAS THIS PRINCE MADOC?

He was more than a legend. He was born in 1150, in Wales. His full name was Madoc ab Owain Gwynedd, son of King Owain Gwynedd, who ruled a Welsh kingdom for 32 years (1138-1169). He was said to have had 17 sons, including Madoc, and at least two daughters – by more than one wife. When the king died in 1169, his sons fought over who should succeed him. Prince Madoc quickly tired of the civil war and in 1170 (some literature says a year earlier) set out in a single ship, the Gwennan Gorn, to find a better, more peaceful place in which to live. Most of the literature agrees that he found Florida, and deemed it an ideal location in which to start a colony. He returned to Wales and organized a flotilla of ten ships, each filled with his fellow countrymen, and in 1170 set forth from the Island of Lundy to start a new life in the new world. None of them ever returned.

Most authorities agree that the Madoc party this time landed in Mobile Bay, Alabama. The flotilla then went up the Alabama River, ending up in what is now Tennessee. From there they supposedly took water routes northwest, eventually navigating the Missouri River. Early explorers found the remains of several fortifications along that route which were likely built by Europeans before explorations by Columbus. There are also scores of reports of early explorers and traders encountering Indians who had Welsh words in their vocabularies. There are reports of Roman coins being found that had been struck in Wales. (this author has not been able to identify what happened to any of these coins or whether they even exist today.) There are also reports of non-Indian skeletons being found along the rivers used by the Welsh.

There are copies still around – but not the original – of a letter written by the first governor of Tennessee, John Sevier, in response to an inquiry from a Major Amos Stoddard who was writing a history of Louisiana. the letter is dated October 9, 1810, and was written in Knoxville:

"sir:

Your letter of Aug. 30 is before me. With respect to the information you have requested, I shall with pleasure give you so far as my own memory will now serve me; and also aided by a memorandum taken on the subject, of a nation of people called the Welsh Indians. In the year 1782 I was on a campaign against some part of the Cherokees; during the route I had discovered traces of very ancient tho' regular fortifications. Some short time after the expedition I had an occasion to enter into a negotiation with the Cherokee Chiefs for the purpose of exchanging prisoners. After the exchange had been settled, I took an opportunity of enquiring of a venerable old chief called Oconostota, who then and had been for nearly sixty years the ruling chief of the Cherokee Nation, if he could inform me what people it had been which had left such signs of Fortifications in their Country and in Pre-Columbian Explorer Sites in the Southeast particularly the one on the bank of Highwassee River. the old chief immediately informed me: "It was handed down by the Forefathers that the works had been made by the white people who had formerly inhabited the Country, and at the same time the Cherokees resided low down in the country now called South Carolina; that a war had existed between the two nations for several years. At length it was discovered that the whites were making a number of large Boats which induced the Cherokees to suppose they were about to descend the Tennessee River. They then assembled their whole band of warriors and took the shortest and most convenient route to the Muscle Shoals in order to intercept them on their passage down the river. In a few days the Boats hove in sight. A warm combat ensued with various success for several days. At length the whites proposed to the Indians that they would exchange prisoners and cease hostilities, they would leave the Country and never more return, which was acceded to; and after the exchange parted friendly. That the whites then descended the Tennessee down to the Ohio, thence down to the big river (the Mississippi) then they ascended it up to the Muddy River (the Missouri) and thence up that river for a great distance. That they were then on some of its branches, but, says he, they are no more a white people; they are now all become Indians, and look like the other red people of the Country.""

"I then asked him if he had ever heard any of his ancestors saying what nation of people these whites belonged to. He answered: "He had heard his Grandfather and Father say they wee a people called Welsh; that they had crossed the Great Water and landed first near the mouth of the Alabama River near Mobile and had been drove up to the heads of the waters until they had arrived at Highwassee River by the Mexican Indians who had been drove out of their own Country by the Spaniards.""

"Many years ago I happened in company with a French-man, who had lived with the Cherokees and said he had formerly been high up the Missouri. He informed me he had traded with the Welsh tribe; that they certainly spoke much of the Welsh dialect and tho' their customs was savage and wild yet many of them, particularly the females, were very fair and white, and frequently told him that they had sprung from a white nation of people. He also stated that some small scraps of old books remained among them, but in such tattered and destructive order that nothing intelligent remained in the pieces or scraps left. He observed, their settlement was in an obscure quarter on a branch of the Missouri running through a bed of lofty mountains. His name has escaped by memory."

"Thee chief Oconostota informed me: "An old woman in his nation called Peg had some part of an old book given her by an Indian who had lived high up the Missouri, and thought it was one of the Welsh tribe." Before I had an opportunity of seeing it, her house and all the contents burnt. I have seen persons who had seen parts of a very old and disfigured book with this old Indian woman, but neither of them could make any discovery of what language it was printed in (neither of them understood languages, but a small smattering of English).

"I have thus, Sir, communicated and detailed the particulars of your request, so far as I have any information on the subject, and wish it were more comprehensive than you will find it written."

Among the most significant pieces of evidence that Prince Madoc and his Welsh followers were in the Alabama - Tennessee - Georgia area more than 300 years before Columbus "discovered" America are three rock walls, totally unlike anything ever built by American Indian tribes. Archeologists have dated the construction as in the 1100s. They surely could have been used for protection, but there has been some speculation that they could also have had some religious function.

The first wall is located at the top of Lookout Mountain near DeSoto Falls, Alabama. Some have likened it to the construction of the castle where Madoc was born in Wales (Dolwyddelan castle in Gwynedd).

Fort Mountain State Park in Northern Georgia.
The wall is all that remains of a huge Welch fortification.

The best preserved and largest of these rock walls is to be found in the Fort Mountain State Park in northern Georgia (many have referred to these walls as forts). This wall is at the highest point of the mountain. It is about seven feet high at its tallest and extends for 885 feet. Originally it could have been much higher. It averages twelve feet in width and there are 29 pits at regular intervals along its length. The wall runs east and west.

The third is called "Old Stone Fort", and is located near Manchester, Tennessee. It is formed by high bluffs and walls as tall as twenty feet. Unique to this fort (of the three forts) is a moat 1200 feet in length. Apart form the walled cities of the Mandans (and their walls were made of wood), there is no Native American construction like any of these walls or forts anywhere in North America. Either they were constructed by a very unique tribe, or – far more likely – were built by Europeans.

As the wall-builders moved west and north they constructed several small, and perhaps temporary, fortifications.

THE NAYSAYERS –

It should come as no surprise that not all authorities, whether historians or archeologists, agree that the evidence we have cited proved there were Welsh colonists in North America prior to the explorations of Columbus. Over the years individuals have questioned whether the white Mandans were part Welsh, whether the Welsh did settle in North America or whether Prince Madoc was more than a legend. It has been suggested that the Madoc legend was concocted to give the British a claim to more of North America. Early European literature, however, leaves little doubt that the story was well know long before the time of Columbus. Ancient authors include Sir Thomas Herbert ("Relation of Some Years of Travail", 1626), Hornius (a Dutch writer) and richard Hakluyt ("Principal Navigations", 1600) – all support the veracity of Prince Madoc's explorations and attempts of colonization in North America.

A Welchman, John Evans, traveled to America in 1792 and spent a winter with the Mandans. He later testified that they did not speak Welsh. George Catlin, however, whose visit with the tribe came later, did point out similarities in certain words in the two languages, saying that several were pronounced exactly the same. Scores of traders and explorers also testified that they encountered other Indians who had Welsh words in their vocabularies. It should not be surprising that after more than six hundred years of inter-marrying of the Welsh and Native Americans that only a few Welsh words remained in their respective vocabularies. What is surprising is that any Welsh words were left at all or that "white characteristics", such as light skin, blue and hazel eyes or every color of hair but red remained! There are also those who believe Evans was paid off by the Spanish to prevent additional claims by the British to western lands. Evans should be credited, however, with charting the Missouri River and some of its tributaries and that this map was helpful to Lewis and Clark.

Clearly there is a large accumulation of evidence that white settlers did come to North America before the Columbus exploration of 1492:

- The Mandan Indians with their "white" physical characteristics, walled cities with streets, comfortable houses, European traditions of how women were treated, etc.,

- The three large, pre-historic rock fortifications in the southeast and several smaller ones along the likely route of the colonists to the west and north,

- Many reports in the early history of our country of encounters with Indians of lighter complexion, even curly hair and some men who had beards and, in addition,

- The many reports of tribes using from a few to many Welsh words.

AND IF NOT THE WELSH, THEN WHO?

CHAPTER THREE

THE VIKINGS

Down through the years we have grown accustomed to calling all of the Scandinavian explorers "Vikings". There truly is a difference between the early adventurers, the true Vikings, who were known to be warlike plunderers and the Norsemen who came later and were quite civilized and who were practicing Christians. The change came during the 11th century.[1] In the text which follows we will use the term "Viking" to describe both, but we will tell you when it is really the Norse we are talking about by adding that word parenthetically, thus: Viking (Norse). the Norse also claimed Iceland, Greenland or their motherland, Norway, as their residence, but there were others who joined them from Sweden and Denmark.

It is well documented that the Vikings of Scandinavia discovered North America approximately 500 years before Columbus saw our shores. Now that we not only have written evidence (Norwegian and Icelandic sagas) that this is true but also have discovered the remains of a Viking village in Newfoundland, it is a little hard to understand why we still teach our school children that Columbus discovered America.

Perhaps an argument can be made that the publicity of the Columbus achievement dramatically changed how Europe looked at the rest of the world, but we still owe it to the Vikings and the Welsh to recognize their earlier discovery.

---

[1] About the year 1070 when the Vikings were defeated by the British.

First, we have the written word as evidence. The Scandinavians called these chronicles "Sagas". There were several origins of these first written accounts but the best known came from Greenland and Iceland. Adam of Bremen, a German religious, also wrote about a North American Viking settlement sometime prior to 1076. We know from these sagas that Norwegian and Danish Vikings launched explorations from their native lands long before they saw the coast of North America. Their relatively small wooden ships, driven by wind and by oars, explored much of the coast of Europe, including the British Isles and going east as far as the Black and Caspian Seas and Constantinople. They had a huge impact on Russian civilization.

Prior to their discovery of North America, these hardy Vikings established actual settlements in the North Atlantic, including the Orkney, Shetland and Faroe Islands between 780 and 800 AD. Eventually, the Vikings' courage and curiosity lead them to Iceland, Greenland and the coast of North America. Iceland was the first to be colonized (870 AD). Thanks to the written sagas of that day we know something about the leaders of these ventures. Eric the Red, whose last name was Thorvaldson, was born in Norway, but his family fled to Iceland after his father was banished from Norway for murdering a man. Eric apparently inherited his father's disposition because he killed two men in Iceland and was banished from that country for three years. As a result, he discovered and named Greenland. The year was 982. He gathered a crew and set sail due west. He first found Gunnbjorn's Islands and then landed on the east coast of Greenland, which was anything but green! Legend has it that he chose this nice but inappropriate name because he hoped to someday attract settlers. He then sailed around the southern tip of Greenland and landed on the southwest coast. He spent the winter on an island, appropriately named "Erik's Island"; he spent the following two years on the southern tip of Greenland. By then his three year sentence was over and he returned to Iceland, where he proved to be an outstanding salesman as he recruited between 400 and 500 individuals to return with him to Greenland in fourteen ships. The year was 986. They settled in two communities: Brattahlid – now called Julianehab - to the west and Gotthab, to the east. It is not known exactly how long they stayed, but many returned to Iceland because of the severe climate and the remnant were apparently killed by the natives or died from disease. Eric died during the winter of 1003-04.

Eric the Red had three sons and a daughter. One son, Lief (the Lucky) Ericsson, also earned fame as an explorer. He visited Norway and was there converted to Christianity. King Olaf directed him to return to Greenland as a missionary to convert those settlers.

On his way back, he encountered a trading vessel that was in danger of foundering and rescued the crew. He was given the cargo as a reward, thereby receiving his nickname "Leif the Lucky". Before reaching Greenland, he was blown off course and ended up on the coast of North America. The year was about 1000 AD., nearly 500 years before Columbus "discovered" America! He is believed to have touched land at Labrador, Newfoundland and the Baffin Islands.

According to the Greenland Saga, Bjarni Herjolfsson was the first to see the coast of North America, in 985 AD, but did not go ashore.

All Sagas referred to an actual settlement known as "Vinland". It is generally believed that the name indicated the presence of wild grapes. We do not know exactly where it was located, but from the descriptions of the area it is thought to have been below the Gulf of St. Lawrence. The leader of this new community was Throfinn Karlsefni. His journals record that a son was born to him and his wife in Vinland. The settlement must have lasted at least three years, because that is how old the boy was when they abandoned the site and returned to Greenland. The Native Americans (the Vikings called them "Skraelings") were not happy to have new neighbors and their frequent attacks on the settlers is cited as the main reason the Vikings (Norse) abandoned the settlement.

Thorvald Erickson (Lief's brother), was involved in one of the skirmishes with the aborigines in which eight Indians were killed. According to several sagas, not all encounters were violent, but the periods of peace were seldom very long.

It is likely that there were several colonies started by the Vikings (Norse) along the Atlantic shore of North America, but the one described as "Vinland" was probably the southern most site and located just below the Gulf of St. Lawrence. It was described in the sagas as rich in wild grapes, timber and self-sown wheat. Grapes would probably not grow in the northern sites. The only site thus far that has been documented by the discovery of ruins and other artifacts is in Newfoundland. It was discovered in 1960 by the Norwegians archaeologists Helge Ingstad and Anne Stine (husband and wife). The settlement was apparently short-lived but provided many valuable artifacts. It is called L'Anse aux Meadows (which translates Meadow Cove). But it does not fit the description of Vinland as portrayed in the Scandinavian sagas.

Excavation has turned up the outlines of eight structures originally made with sod walls. One of the buildings was apparently a bath house very similar to those constructed in Norse villages in Greenland. A smithy was also excavated. Other artifacts include iron nail fragments, a copper alloy, ring headed pin (used to secure clothing), a spindle made of soapstone, a lamp made of stone, wooden patches used to repair boats and wood fragments of unknown purpose.

The following pictures were furnished by the Canadian National Parks service.

Aerial view of the settlement.

Reconstructed woven fence around buildings.

The excavated smithy.

Interior view of the restored longhouse, left; a fireplace in the longhouse, right.

EARLY MAPS

THE VINLAND MAP – Courtesy of Beinecke Rare Book andManuscript Library, Yale University

THE STEFFANSON MAP – 16th Century map of Western Europe and Eastern North America
Courtesy of Beinecke Rare Book andManuscript Library, Yale University

The Vinland Map may be the oldest map of North America. It may have been first published around 1440 AD. We say "may" because its authenticity has been challenged. The map was first discovered bound in an old book and brought to light in 1965. It is the property of Yale University. The university claimed it was for real – and still does. However, in 1972, a team of scientists headed by Dr. Walter NcCrone found that the ink contained anatase, an ingredient that was supposedly not used in ink prior to the 1920s. But in 1992, Dr. Thomas Cahill of the University of California (at Davis), discovered anatase in several medieval manuscripts.

Other challenges have followed, almost too numerous to mention, but most, if not all, of the questions raised have been answered. If the debate is of interest to you, I suggest you read the research published in 2005 by J. Huston McCulloch. All 50 pages of his study may be found on the internet. Look in Google under the topic: "Vinland map" and click on McCulloch's study. He takes on all challenges and concludes with this statement: "The fact that it has resisted all arguments against it over the past four decades makes it begin to appear genuine after all…"

It is interesting that the east coast of North America (including Vinland) is portrayed as an island only a little larger than Greenland, (far left on the map).

The writing above Vinland and Greenland has been translated as: 'By God's will, after a long voyage from the island of Greenland to the south toward the most distant remaining parts of the western ocean sea, sailing southward amidst the ice, the companions Bjarni and Lief Eriksson discovered a new land, extremely fertile and even having vines, which island they named Vinland. Eric (Henricus), legate of the Apostolic See and Bishop of Greenland and the neighboring regions, arrived in this vast and very rich land, in the name of Almighty God, in the last year of our most blessed Father Pascal, remained a long time in both summer and winter, and later returned northeastward toward Greenland and then proceeded in most humble obedience to the will of his Superior."

I don't think I would want to navigate by this map! In all fairness, however, the European portion of the map is much more accurate which is not surprising since the Vikings had sailed those waters often – and for many years.

The lower map on page 64 was drawn by a Norwegian teacher, Sigurd Stefansson, in the 1500s and is based on Icelandic writings rather than navigational experience. The map assumes that the Atlantic Ocean is bordered on the north by a continuous coastline, thus Greenland is shown as part of the continent. Vining (and Newfoundland and Labrador) is located in the lower left-hand corner of the map.

VIKING (NORSE) PENETRATIONS OF THE NORTH AMERICAN MAINLAND

There is no longer any question about the Vikings (and Norse[1]) exploring and establishing settlements on the east coast of the continent. The sagas of Iceland and Greenland were credible evidence but the discovery of the remains of an actual settlement in Newfoundland removed all doubt. The question remaining is: Did the Vikings (Norse) explore the interior of the continent and, if so, how far did their explorations penetrate?

There are three significant pieces of evidence that the Vikings (Norse) did penetrate the interior but thus far there is not total agreement on their authenticity:

1. The Peterborough Petroglyphs
2. The Kensington Runestone
3. The Heavener Runestone

THE PETERBOROUGH PETROGLYPHS

The site contains about 2,500 square feet of approximately 900 carvings in relatively soft, white limestone and is located near Peterborough, Ontario. The site was buried, either accidentally or on purpose, and was not discovered and uncovered until 1954. Archeologists have dated the glyphs as sometime between 900 and 1400 AD. Although carved in relatively soft stone it is likely that they were drawn with iron tools. There are 15 human figures and 14 canoes and boats.

The site is located along the most common canoe route used by Native Americans and early whites for east-west travel, through Georgian Bay via the Trent and Severn Rivers. It is conceivable that the carvings were made by a great variety of artist over a long period of time.

The possible Viking (and/or Norse) connection is in the pictures of boats, most of which are not at all like the canoes used by Indian tribes of that part of the continent. Several ships are very similar to those used by Vikings (and/or Norse). the accompanying picture is a replica of the largest boat carving – three and one-half feet long. The unique features of an

---

[1] The Norse Vikings were Catholic and totally different from the earlier Vikings who were barbaric plunderers.The change came during the 15th century when Christianity came to the Scandinavian countries.

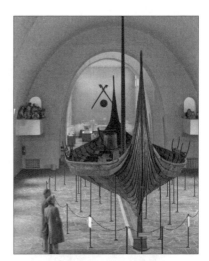

The largest drawing of a ship among those appearing in the Peterborough petroglyphs. (3 1/2 feet long)

Salvaged Viking Ship
Olso Viking Museum

animal-headed prow and tall mast topped by a circle characterized a Viking (Norse) vessel. The radiating circle on top of the mast represents the Virgin Mary and is a symbol of her protection. It is believed that the mast was sometimes removed and carried in processions when the Vikings traveled on foot. What we don't know, of course, is whether smaller ships actually traveled this route or if they were seen along the coast and just portrayed here.

It is believed that the Vikings (and Norse) carried tools and materials with them for constructing smaller boats, some of which could be portaged.

It is also not known whether the artists were European or Native American or both. Since it is likely that iron tools were used and since the pictures pre-date whites trading with Indians, a good case can be made that at least some of the drawings were by Vikings (Norse) themselves.

Although there is no "proof positive", the Peterborough Petroglyphs remain a significant piece of evidence that the Vikings (Norse) did penetrate the North American continent at least this far.

THE KENSINGTON RUNESTONE

If the Kensington Runestone is authentic, then we have "proof positive" that the Vikings (Norse) did explore more than a third of the way into the continent – more than 100 miles west of Lake Superior.[1] The word "runes" refers to the alphabet used by Scandinavians at the time the Vikings and Norse were exploring the oceans.

Bill Hoyt developed a website which, in our estimation, tells best the story of the Kensington Runestone, including the critical arguments for and against its authenticity. When he was no longer able to maintain the website, Epigraph Forum volunteered to continue the site in its original state. The following is taken from that website:

Al Seltz (left) and Eldon Kratzke view the hill-side site where the Kensington Ruenstone was discovered by Olaf Ohman on November 8, 1898.

The actual ruenstone is on display in a museum in Alexandria, Minnesota – near the small town of Kensington, close to where it was found.

KENSINGTON RUNESTONE
HOME PAGE ON THE INTERNET

"Eight Goths and 22 Norwegians on a journey of exploration from Vinland very far west. We had camp by two rocky islands one day's journey north from this stone. We were out fishing one day. After we came home we found ten men red with blood and dead. AVM save from evil. Have ten men by the sea to look after our ships fourteen days' journey from this island. Year 1362."

---

[1] Unless the stone was carried by Indians to the Kensington location.

"In the 100 years since its discovery, few items have provoked as much scholarly debate as the Kensington Runestone."

"If genuine, it would open a completely new chapter in our understanding of medieval history. It would mean that not only did the Norse explore far wider areas of the North American continent than was previously supposed, but that the Norse era of exploration lasted centuries longer than historians have believed."

"If fraudulent, it is one of the finest hoaxes on record, for not only did it outlive the festers, but their children and (in many cases) their grandchildren as well, with no sign of abating soon."

"FREQUENTLY ASKED QUESTIONS (FAQ)
WHAT IS THE KENSINGTON RUNESTONE?

The Kensington Runestone is a slab of Graywacke stone, grey in color, measuring 36 inches long, 16 inches wide, and 6 inches thick. It contains runic writing along the face of the stone and along one edge. The stone was found on the property of a Minnesota farmer named Olaf Ohman in November of 1898. Upon finding the stone, Mr. Ohman and his sons noted the runic letters, but could not decipher them. The stone was thereafter examined by many runic scholars, who discovered that the runes claimed to be an account of Norse explorers in the 14th Century. Many scholars who have since examined the stone have claimed it a childish forgery; some have testified to its authenticity. The stone currently resides in the Runestone Museum in Alexandria, Minnesota, the seat of the county in which the stone was found."

"What does the inscription say?

The inscription is in 2 parts. The portion on the face of the stone says:

Eight Goths and 22 Norwegians on a journey of exploration from Vinland very far west. We had camp by two rocky islands one day's journey north from this stone. We were out fishing one day. After we came home we found ten men red with blood and dead. AVM save from evil.

The portion along the edge of the stone says:

Have ten men by the sea to look after our ships fourteen days' journey from this island. Year 1362.

The inscription, if genuine, would be one of the longest ancient runic inscriptions in the world. It is certainly one of the most controversial."

"How and where was it found?

On November 8, 1898, a farmer named Olaf Ohman, several of his sons, and some men from neighboring farms were clearing lumber and pulling stumps in preparation for plowing. Ohman was having considerable difficulty digging one tree, a poplar estimated to be between 10 and 40 years old, which was on the southern slope of a 50-foot knoll between his farm and that of Nils Flaaten, Ohman's closet neighbor. When the tree was finally uprooted, the cause of Ohman's trouble came into view: entwined in the roots of the aspen was a 200 pound slab of Graywacke, the Kensington Runestone. The roots of the tree, especially the largest root, were flattened by contact with the stone, as was noted by several people who were there and by later visitors to the site. The stone was found face down in the soil, about six inches below ground level."

"Where has it been since?

The history of the stone since Ohman found it has been an interesting one. After the initial discovery of the stone, it was sent to the University of Minnesota for scholars to examine. The stone made its way to Chicago, where several Swedish, Danish, and Norwegian scholars declared it a fraud of recent date. The stone was then returned to Mr. Ohman, who put it to use as a doorstep for his granary.

In 1907, a young scholar named Hjalmar R. Holand purchased the stone from Mr. Ohman and began to promote it, giving speeches and writing books about the stone, Viking settlements in America, and the "Holy Mission" of Paul Knutson, which supposedly left the stone behind.

For most of 1948 the stone was on exhibit at the Smithsonian Institution, where the curator and director publicly praised it as 'probably the most important archeological object yet found in North America.'

The stone was returned to Minnesota in March of 1949 to be unveiled in St. Paul in honor of the state's centennial. In August it came to a permanent home in Alexandria, Minnesota, at the Runestone Museum, where it resides to this day."

"Are secret "messages" hidden in the inscription?

Several authors, especially the late Alf Monge (a cryptologist with the U.S. Signal Corps during WWII) claim to have "deciphered" secret messages in the runic inscriptions on the Kensington Runestone (and others) and discovered a wealth of information from the name of the person who carved them to the date they were carved to perpetual religious calendars.

Monge gives the following dates for various runic inscriptions:

• Kensington Runestone – April 24th, 1362

• Heavener Runestone – November 11th, 1012

• Poteau Runestone – November 11th, 1017

• Shawnee Runestone – November 24th, 1024

• Tulsa Runestone – December 2nd, 1022

It should be noted that none of these dates has been (or perhaps can be) independently verified."

"Is the runestone genuine?

'We can confidently say that the authenticity of the Kensington Runestone... has been established. The battle is essentially in the past.' – Orval Friedrich, 1986

'From the very beginning the Kensington inscription was recognized by linguistic scholars on both sides of the Atlantic as a simple...modern forgery.' – Eric Wahlgren, 1986

There are three possibilities concerning the authenticity of the stone:

The first is that it is a modern forgery, that the runic inscriptions were carved upon the stone 500+ years after the 1362 date claimed by the inscription. This is the camp in which most linguists and scholars reside, and they cite several good reasons why the inscription cannot be genuine:

- The word opdagelsefard (voyage of discovery) did not occur in the language until several centuries after the 1392 date in the inscription.

- The calendar is not dated to important events, as most runic inscriptions are.

- The inscription uses the English word dead (spelled "ded" in the inscription).

- There are some differences between the stone and various copies of it, leading some to speculate that the "copies" are actually drafts of the jape.[1]

- Finally, the face of the stone is unweathered, and the carving is crisp, hence there is no way it could have remained in the open for even a few years.

Samuel Eliot Morison has written, "Common sense should dismiss this as a hoax...Norsemen were sea discoverers, not land explorers; what possible object could they have had in sailing into Hudson Bay, or through Lake Superior to the portage, and striking out into the wilderness?"

A good question, and one that leads us to our second possibility: that the stone is genuine, and was actually carved by Norsemen in 1362, but in a spot other than where it was found. In other words, the Norsemen in question may not have even been in Minnesota at all. Where it was originally carved is, of course, pure speculation, as there are not many evidences of Vikings anywhere in North America as late as the 14th Century. However, the story becomes a lot more plausible for some if the massacre occurred in Maine or Newfoundland. How the stone got into Ohman's swamp is anybody's guess.

The third possibility is that the stone is what it claims to be: the witness of a lone party of thirty Norse explorers in the middle of North America in 1362. Several facts about the location and discovery of the stone lend weight to this possibility.

- The tree under which the stone was found shows evidence of long contact with the stone. This is important in that if the tree were 40 years old, the stone would had to have been placed in the ground before there were any whites in the area.

---

[1] The word "jape" means "fake" or "hoax."

- The knoll on which it was found could have been an island at one time, as it rose at least 50 feet above the surrounding swamp. Assuming that the water table was different in Minnesota 600 years ago, the argument that significant portions of the area were submerged is not unthinkable.

- Ohman himself never tried to make any money off the stone. In fact, he sold it for but a few bucks. If he were trying to perpetrate a fraud, it can be argued, why did he not ask for more money?

- The prayer to Mary (AVM, or Ave Maria) is thoroughly Catholic, even though the Swedes of Minnesota are overwhelmingly Lutheran. The Swedes of the 14th Century, on the other hand, were Catholic.

- There are scholars who attest to its integrity. While this is not proof, per se, it does show that the inscription is not blatantly spurious in the unanimous opinion of scholarship."

"What was the "Holy Mission"?

According to Holand, a Swede named Paul Knutson was sent in 1354 by King Magnus Ericcson of Sweden and Norway to discover why settlements in Greenland were disappearing, and to bring some Pagans into the Catholic fold. Arriving in Greenland, Knutson found nothing but a few cattle, no settlement was in sight. Again, according to Holand, the mission then continued west to Vinland, and west from Vinland, entering Hudson Bay and traveling up the Nelson River and the Red River (into Minnesota), then the Buffalo River to establish a camp at Lake Cormorant. The party was attacked by Pagan Vikings (rather than the usually-blamed Indians) at that site. The remnants of the party then fled south and carved the runestone on the "island" where it was discovered by Farmer Ohman. Knutson himself never returned, although seven men (including navigator Nicholas of Lynn) are claimed to have made it back to Europe.

"Are there other runestones in America?

There are many claims of other runestones, along with assorted relics and "mooring holes" found in areas of Minnesota, Iowa, and South Dakota, lending evidence to the idea that there were significant Norse incursions into the continent. The relics include halberds, battle axes, spears, and boat hooks. Many of the relics have been claimed by critics to be modern items mistaken for ancient relics, although some (like the "Beardmore Relics") are know to be ancient, but are claimed to have been planted in order to fool the gullible.

The mooring holes are a different story, however. Mooring holes are holes in large boulders into which the Vikings dropped a peg, attached to the ship, to "anchor" it to the shore. Friedrich claims that more than 200 such holes have been found, from South Dakota to Michigan, and that they show that there was a significant Viking presence in North America from about 1000 to 1400. Critics argue that the holes were drilled by modern folk for blasting, but Friedrich argues, who would go to the trouble of drilling a blasting hole and then fail to blast it? Also, drilled holes are round with "V" shaped bottoms, while the mooring holes are rounded triangles with "U" shaped bottoms.

On the subject of runestones, there is one which is worth mentioning: the "Heavener Runestone" of Oklahoma. The Heavener Runestone is a slab about 12 feet high, 10 feet wide, and 16 inches thick with runic letters spelling out the word "Gaomedat". By reversing two runes which appear to be different from the others, the inscription becomes "Golmedal", or "Glome's Valley". I could also be rendered "G. Nomedal", Nomedal being a Norwegian family name.

Several smaller runestones are claimed to have been found (Poteau, Shawnee, Tulsa, all found in the area of Heavener, Oklahoma), although none so famous (or controversial) as the Kensington or Heavener stones."

Answers to Specific Criticisms of the Stone

Most of the criticisms of the authenticity of the runestone (rightly) lie with the inscription itself. If it is a hoax, all of the hoaxers (and probably their children, as well) are now dead, so we are left with only the stone itself to testify to its authenticity (or lack thereof). I hope, in this section, to lay out some of the more famous criticisms of the stone, most notably those which can be checked by research. Some, due to the subjective nature of the argument or the lack of source material, cannot be answered completely. Also, since many scholars make the same objections, I will note only one scholar for each objection, though I may have to quote several in the answer. This is not done to "drive" the reader to an opinion, but only to prove as full an answer as possible to the objection. Notes of quotations will appear at the bottom of the page so as to make the reading of the page easier.

The Language of the Inscription

Objection: "Numerals, in the rare cases in which they appear at all, are cumbrously written out or, in late times, expressed in Roman style. The astonishing thing here is the use of seven numerals or sets of numerals, including the date, all expressed in symbols purporting to be runes, but with place value based on the Hindu-Arabic system of notation, a system that could not possibly mix with runes." (1)

Answer: "The decimal system was of comparatively recent introduction into the North in the XIV century. The most common style then was to state the year of the king's reign…if Anno domini enumeration was used it was usually given in Roman numerals…Another not infrequent method of giving the date was by writing it out in the historical style as is sometimes done now…

Dates in decimal notations are to be found in the Swedish *diplomataria* of the same period. A letter written by a German residing in Sweden begins "int jair ons Heren 1352"…Abundant evidence of the knowledge and use of the decimal system in the XIV is found in several Icelandic annals of the Middle Ages. *Annales Vetussitissimi*, which comes to a close in the year 1314, contains numerous dates and numbers written in decimal notation…*Skalholts Analler*,…contains scores of dates written in decimal notation. *Rymbegla*, a manuscript of about 1300, has many numbers in decimal notation." (18)

It should be noted that none of the inscriptions noted by Holand above are runic. However, it was Holand's contention that the inscriber used runes because they were more easily carved in stone, and used those forms which were most familiar. There is no written rule that the Arabic system cannot be used with runes (at least that I've seen), and the writer was apparently familiar with decimal notation and found it more fitting to carving than writing out the year in a form which would add to his work.

Objection: "A more plausible argument is the claim that the language of the inscription, phonetically, is too modern to be of the 14th Century. It does not sound like the hundreds of letters that have survived from that period." (13)

Answer: "This is quite true, but these letters do not truly represent the speech of the people. In the Middle Ages there were very few people who could read or write. The bishops were therefore instructed to appoint one or more of the monks to act as a *notarii publicii* in each district to draw up contracts, conveyances of sale, or testamentary gifts to the Church, for a fixed compensation, These scriveners constituted a professional class who took their accomplishments very seriously. In order to impress the common people with their learning and dignity, they adopted a stilted style based on the more sonorous language of the past. Aside from the names, the opening sentence was always the same: *"Ollum Monnum beim som sea eda hojra betta bref senda Paal Jonsson og Peter Berg quedia gudh ok sina."* Then follow the details in as antique a wording as possible. Thus, the notaries gave the parties concerned an assurance that the document was drawn up in the most approved and time-honored form and was therefore above reproach and fully dependable, just as many legal documents, even now, are drawn up in clumsy and well-nigh obsolete language.

This antiquated style was favored by the scriveners into the 16th Century, although it is recognized by many philologists that linguistically it was a thing of the past even in the 14th Century. Professor Munch, writing of the 14th Century, says:

The melodious and highly infected Old Norse language was being displaced by a less elegant transition language, marked by lacerated verb forms and the lack of strict grammatical rules, and was therefore not written the same way by any two writers...The regular grammatical inflections which distinguish all old languages were the first to be discarded...The neglect of inflection endings and the substitution of particles or the use of certain modified sentence structures became characteristic. (14)

The fact is that all these meticulous examinations of the inscription have failed to produce any evidence that it could not have been written in the 14th Century. There are certain peculiarities - misspelled words, lax phonetics, and doubtful grammar - but there are none which can be proven incompatible with oral usage at the time of the date it carries, which was before the printed page began to standardize the language. Thalbitzer, O.I. Hagen, S.N. Hagen, Soderwall, Lindroth, Indrebo, and Fossum, all recognized Scandinavian philologists, have found no reason to doubt the authenticity of the inscription because of linguistic difficulties." (13)

Objection: "The amusing language of the inscription includes the English word "dead" (spelled DED)..." (2)

Answer: "Ded. Most critics believe this is a misspelling of the English word *dead*. They point to it as an illustration of the tendency of immigrants in America to mix English words with their native speech. It is true that such mixing is common, but there is a certain system about it. Words pertaining to their daily life such as farm, barn, stable, dinner, bedroom, factory, good time, etc., are quickly adopted into their native speech, but this is not the case with sacred or serious words such as God, saviour, church, death, government, etc. This is a rule I have never heard violated. Professor Kock has given a much better and no doubt correct explanation of *ded* for *dod* (the "o" has the sound of "u" in urn). He points out in his history of Swedish phonetics that there was in the Middle Ages a frequent substitution of e for o, such as in *hera* for *hora*, *breder for broder*, *lena for lona*, *grea for groa*, etc. (7) Rydquist also gives a large number of illustrations of this tendency. (8) In a letter written in 1390 by Queen Margaret we find two examples of this. One is her spelling of the name of Lodose (she spells it *Ledese*). The other is her spelling of the same word which is criticized in the inscription. The sentence reads: 'Effther the henne husbonde her Jens Herne ded er' = 'because her husband, Sir Jense Herne, is dead.' (9) Opponents of the inscription dispose of this annoying comparison by saying that the Queen (or her secretary) made a mistake. But if the writer of the letter could make a mistake, why could not also the writer of the inscription?" (10)

Objection: "one word alone, opdagelsefard, which did not appear in any Scandinavian language for several centuries after 1362, gives it away."

Objection: "The most criticized word in the inscription is opdagelse. This word, it is claimed, is an anachronism. It could not have been used in 1362 because it is not found in Soderwall's dictionary of medieval Swedish.

It is an error to conclude that a word did not exist in the medieval Swedish if it is not found in this excellent dictionary. As Professor Soderwall did not live in the Middle Ages, his only sources about Sweden's medieval vocabulary were the preserved books and documents of that period. This literature was rather limited in scope, and there are many words he did not include in his dictionary because they were not mentioned in the old writings. As an example, there is the word, *eldstal* (fire steel), which was used in the flint-and-fire-steel process of making fire. This steel was an implement no house in the Middle Ages could be without. But it is not mentioned by Soderwall because it does not occur in the old writings, which are mostly conveyances of land.

Professor Soderwall had no doubt that *obdage* was in use in the 14th Century. I spent a couple of hours with him in his study, and he gave me the following statement:

'As far as I know, this word is not to be found in the meager literary fragments of the 14th Century. But that proves nothing. As you probably know, these fragments consist chiefly of legal documents and homilies, and it is therefore not strange if a word of such comparably rare import is *obdagelse* is not found in such writings. The old Norse word for this idea was *Leita Landa*, but this expression had become obsolete when the great change from Old Swedish to the Swedish of the late Middle Ages took place about 1300. As landelieta was dropped, some other term must have been adopted to express the same thought. The only word we know which fills this function is opdage.'" (6)

The Runic Characters

Objection: "The Latin phrase AVM is modern, and is evidence that Ohman, who had a scrapbook with buddhist notes in it, carved the inscription: he (Wahlgren) called special attention to the syllable AUM at the end of the note on Buddah and pointed out its resemblance to AVM on the rune stone. (19)

The forms of these letters have been severely criticized by the eminent archaeologist, Professor Ocar Montelius, on the grounds that such unornamented gothic forms were not in use in the fourteenth century." (20)

Answer: "If the inscription were written on parchment in a quiet monastery, this criticism would be very much to the point, for it is true that the majuscule were very much in vogue among the clerks of the fourteenth century. We also find them generally used by the artistic engravers of seals. But if the Kensington Runestone is genuine, it was written under quite other circumstances...as a pious Catholic, he felt it incumbent to show his reverence for the holy name of the Virgin by writing it in the capitol letters of the Church, but even then he only takes time for the first letter of each syllable. Circumstances were not propitious for further elaboration.

If the majuscule used by the clerks were different in *type* from the Gothic, the criticism would be valid...The basic Gothic form is and was easily recognized in all majuscule, and such unornamented forms occur quite frequently among them. Three of four instances may be cited:

The seal of Ingeger Philipsdatter, widow of the knight Magnum Gregerson, from 1326, reads:

(S' IN) GI (GER) DIS FILIE PHILLIPI in practically plain Gothic forms.

The gravestone of Ragnild, the daughter of the priest Jon, from ca. 1350, contains the words A VE Maria in almost pure Gothic forms.

A seal of 1330 shows all three letters (A V M) in unornamented forms.

In the Bergen, Norway, museum is a seal of the Rostock from the fourteenth or fifteenth century which contains only plain Gothic letters." (20)

The Stone and Circumstances of its Discovery

Objection: "Unlike genuine medieval rune stones, this one presents a smooth and relatively unweathered face." (2)

Answer: "If the stone was a hoax, the face of the stone should be *completely* unweathered, as it would have taken many years of exposure to the elements for the runes to assume the weathered appearance they now have. However, since it was found face down in the ground, there is no reason to believe it should appear as weathered as those runestones which have been exposed to the elements for centuries.

This is a very hard stone which weathers slowly, but many geologists have called attention to the fact that the inscribed characters in this area show a weathering which is just as marked as the uninscribed area of the stone. A sample of these is Dr. Upham's statement. He says:

'When we compare the excellent preservation of the glacial scratches shown on the back of the stone, which were made several thousand years ago, with the mellow, time-worn appearance of the face of the inscription, the conclusion is inevitable that this inscription must have been made many hundreds of years ago.' (3)

In the lower left corner of the inscribed area is seen a lighter colored surface. This is a layer of calcite. this softer stone has been so corroded by rain, after the inscription was made, as to remove a sizeable layer of its surface. In fact, it is so worn down that some of the characters have been obliterated and can only be read by help of context. In most photographs they show up more plainly because the runes have usually been traced over with a pencil to make them readable." (4)

Objection: "Most damning of all were several contemporary paper texts purporting to be copies from the stone, but comparative study of which indicates that they were experimental variants, or rough drafts, of a proposed inscription, made by one or more persons involved in promoting the hoax. In brief, they *anteceded* the actual carving." (2)

Answer: "This objection was first raised by Erik Moltke, upon reviewing a report by John A. Holvik, a Lutheran seminary student who was involved in one of the original inspections of the stone. It is to Moltke's work which Holand responds below:

'Holvik claims that the 'runepaper', or 'draft', as he calls it, contains seven words using different rune-forms from those on the stone. He also finds seven words showing differences in spelling.

It is not easy to copy a long document containing strange characters without making mistakes, a fact well illustrated by Professor Oluf Rygh of Oslo University, who in 1899 attempted to copy the inscription from a print form. In this I think he had an advantage over Ohman, because Rygh had the print form on his desk, while Ohman could not get the stone so close. Yet Rygh makes more mistakes than Ohman. (11) I quote below Holvik's and Moltke's reasons for believing that Ohman's 'runepaper' is a draft and not a copy of the inscription. Alternating with them are Rygh's mistakes.

'1. On the runepaper the word for *from* is written *FRO* the first time it appears and FROM in the fourth line, while the stone has *FRO* in both places.' Rygh makes precisely the same mistake.

'2. On the runepaper the word for *rod* is written with an H-rune after the vowel. There is no H-rune in the same word on the stone.' Rygh again makes the same mistake and in addition makes two more on the same word. He spells it *rohde*; it should be rode.

'3. The word for blood is spelled with a complicated character for the umlaut of O, which is an incorrect spelling in any Scandinavian language at any time.'

This is quite true; no one drafting an inscription would write *blo(umlaut)d* because there is no such word. It shows that the copyist did not understand the runes and made a mistake.

As these three examples are all that Holvik and Moltke give, it may be presumed that they are the most damning. But so far one might just as well claim that Rygh's transcription was a draft as much as Ohman's supposed runepaper. In the first and second criticized words both men made the same mistake, and the third is plainly not part of a draft as Holvik has shown.

There are other proofs that Ohman's runepaper was a copy and not a draft of the inscription. One is found on the first line (figure is noted-ed). It will be seen that the last four letters have been rubbed out and then rewritten in the next line. There must have been some reason for this. If the runepaper was written as a draft there was no reason for rubbing them out because there is no change in the letters and there was plenty of room. But if the runepaper is a *copy* of the inscription we see why these letters were moved to the next line. The copyist evidently planned to make an exact copy, line for line, of the inscription. Too late he discovered that these four letters belonged on the second line, and he therefore erased them. But soon he found it too difficult to duplicate the spacing on the stone, and then used his own spacing. As in the inscription, he did manage to get his copy into twelve lines." (12)

The Library of Olaf Ohman

Objection: "It has been alleged by several writers, notably Wahlgren (15) and Blegen (16) that Olaf Ohman had in his library sources which would enable him (assuming he was the forger) to create the stone. In Ohman's small library were two books, *Den Kunskapsrike Skolmasteren* ("the Well-Informed Schoolmaster" – by Carl Rosander and Oscar Montelius' *Swedish History*, which these authors mainly cite.

Rosander contains several runes, all of which appear in the runestone in differing forms. After quoting the passage *AVM fraelse af illu*, Wahlgren exclaims, 'Comparing the phrase on the Kensington stone with the parallel in Roseander, it is obvious we need to look no further.'

Of this, Pohl says: 'Wahlgren's argument would be greatly strengthened if the much-disputed expression AVM could have been found by Ohman ready-made in Rosander. He therefore ventured to put it in Roasnder!

In his Index, p. 223, Wahlgren has this entry: 'AVM: in Rosander, 137.' It is unde-niable that the letters *A, V,* and *M* do appear on many pages of Rosander, but unfortunately for Professor Wahlgren they never appear consecutively in that order. The expression AVM is not in Rosander.

The fact is that is Rosander there are only 13 of the 30 symbols in the Kensington inscription. The symbols in that inscription which are not in Rosander are the nine runes for *U (W, V), Y (J), P, O, A, AE, U, K,* and *G;* the expression *AVM,* and the seven numerals. (17)

On the possibility that Ohman might have read that Swedes and Norwegians traveled together (8 *Goths and 22 Norwegians,* from the Runestone inscription), Pohl says: 'Actually, there is nothing in the section on Swedish history in Rosander, or in *Swedish History*...which would give information that Goths and Norwegians travelled together in the 1360s when King Magnus of Norway for a time ruled over the Swedish province of Westgothland." (17)

ENDNOTES

Many of the following notes are cited in other works listed here. If I have not personally checked the references, I will list the work the reference is cited in by "cited in".

1. **Wahlgren, Erik,** *The Vikings and America*
   Thames and Hudson, 1986, p. 102

2. ibid., p. 103

3. Statement on file in the archives of the Minnesota Historical Society - cited in (4).

4. **Holand, H.R.,** *Explorations in America Before Columbus*
   Twayne Publishers, 1956, pp. 171-172

5. **Morison, Samuel Eliot,** *The European Discovery of America*
   Oxford University Press, 1971, p. 77

6. **Holand, H.R.,** *Explorations in America before Columbus*
   Twayne Publishers, 1956, pp. 314-315

7. **Koch, Axel,** *Svensk Ljudhistoria, II*, pp. 38-42, cited in (10)

8. *Svenska Sprakets Lagar, IV*, pp. 98-101 - cited in (10)

9. *Diplamatarium Norwegicum*, Vol. 4, no. 586 - cited in (10)

10. **Holand, H.R.,** *Explorations in America before Columbus*
    Twayne Publishers, 1956, p. 318

11. *Morgenbladet,* 1899

12. **Holand, H.R.,** *Explorations in America before Columbus*
    Twayne Publishers, 1956, pp. 339-340

13. **Holand, H.R.,** *Explorations in America before Columbus*
    Twayne Publishers, 1956, pp. 321-324

14. *Dip Nor.,* Vol. IV, no. 501 - cited in (13)

15. **Wahlgren, Erik,** *The Kensington Stone, A Mystery Solved*
    University of Wisconsin Press, 1958, p. 137 - cited in (17)

16. **Blegen, Theodore,** *The Kensington Stone, New Light on an Old Riddle*
    Minnesota Historical Society, 1968

17. **Pohl, Frederick,** *Atlantic Crossings Before Columbus*
    W.W. Norton and Company, 1961, pp.223-224

18. **Holand, H.R.,** *The Kensington Stone*
    Private Printing, 1932, pp.254-256

19. **Blegen, Theodore,** *The Kensington Stone, New Light on an Old Riddle*
    Minnesota Historical Society, 1968, p. 75

20. **Holand, H.R.,** *The Kensington Stone*

"The following .gif is taken from the Norwegian Skepis Magazine, Winter 94/95.

ᛒ᛬ᚤᚯᛏᛏᚱ᛬ᛏᛏ᛬ᚠᚠᛘᚱᚱᚤᛏᛏᛒᛏ᛬
ᛁ᛬ᛂᛒᚦᚷᚤᛏᚴᚤᛏᚠᚷᚱᛚ᛬ᚠᚱᛏ᛬
ᚤᛁᛏᚠᚷᛏᚦᛂᚠ᛬ᚤᛏᚴᛏᛁᚤᛁ᛬

ᛏᚷᛒᛏ᛬ᚴᚯᚤᛏᚱ᛬ᚤᛏᚦ᛬ᚠ᛬ᚴᛏᚠᚷᚱ᛬ᛏᛏ᛬
ᚦᚷᚤᚴ᛬ᚱᛁᚴᛏ᛬ᛏᚱᚱ᛬ᚠᚱᛏᚦᛏᛏᚴᛏᛏ᛬
ᚤᛁᚤᚷᚱᛏᛏ᛬ᚠᛁᚴᛏᛏᛏᛏᚦᚷᚤᛏᚯᛒᛏᛁᚱ᛬

ᚤᛁ᛬ᛏᛂᚤ᛬ᛏᛏᚤ᛬ᚠᚷᛏᛌᚤ᛬ᚤᚷᛏᚱᚯᚦᛏ᛬
ᚷᚠᛒᚴᛏᚦᛂᚤ᛬ᚦᛏᚦᛌAᚢᛗ᛬
ᚠᚱᚷᛏᚴᛏᚷᚠᛁᛁᛌᚤ

Transliteration: The runes found on the side of the stone make up the bottom three lines of the above inscription. the words on the stone are separated by dots (:), which have not been included below. All transliterations and translations are apt to differ slightly.

Front: 8 goter ok 22 norrmen pa opdagelsefard fra winland of west wi hade lager wed 2 skjar en dags rise norr fra dena sten wi war ok fiske en dagh aptir wi kom hem fan 10 man rode af blod og ded AVM

Side: har 10 mans we hawet at se aptir wore skip 14 dagh rise fram dena oh ahr 1362

Translation: Front: 8 Goths (Swedes) and 22 Norwegians on a voyage of discovery from Vinland of the West. We had a camp by 2 skerries one day journey north from this stone. We were out fishing one day. After we came home we found 10 men red with blood and dead. AVM (Ave Virgin Mary) save (us) from evil.

Side: (We) have 10 men of (ours) by the sea to look after our ships 14 day journeys north from this island. Year 1362."

END OF QUOTE FROM THE WEBSITE

THE HEAVENER RUNESTONE

A number of stones have been discovered in North America that have runic lettering carved in them, but in nearly every case it is only a few letters - too few to decipher a message. We spoke earlier of a stone discovered by Pierre LeVerendrye in his travels, but that was given to the Jesuits and has somehow been lost. (It truly would be interesting if he found it while visiting the Mandans!:) There are two runestones other than the one found near Kensington, Minnesota, that have enough recognizable characters to deliver a message, and they were found near Heavener, Oklahoma.

The Heavener Runestone has been a mystery ever since the first whites settled in that area. They took the lettering to have been carved by Native Americans and called it "Indian Rock". The letters are carved on a huge slab, 12 feet tall, 10 feet wide and 16 inches thick. Gloria Farley identified the carvings as Scandinavian runes and has translated the message as "Gnomel's Valley". Ms. Farley poured 33 years of research into the project and was instrumental in persuading the Oklahoma legislature to establish a state park at the site.

Farley concluded that Vikings discovered the mouth of the Mississippi River and followed that steam north to the Arkansas and then the Poteau Rivers. She further theorizes that the Vikings may have settled at or near the site for a time.

If the rock does, indeed, name the valley for someone called "Gonomel", no one knows who that might have been – maybe a Viking Chief.

The Smithsonian has verified that the characters are runes.

Alf Monge, a Norwegian cryptanalyst, believed the runes represented the date November 11, 1012.[1]

Four smaller, additional runestones have been found in the area, all in a straight line. The Poteau Stone has been translated by Dr. Robert Nielsen (who earned his degree at the University of Denmark) as "magic (or protection) to Golie" (possibly Glomedal's nickname). The Shawnee Stone has the name "Medok" on it – possibly a headstone, but indications are it may have been moved during some construction. The other two stones do not have enough characters for any translation. The Shawnee Stone may have been moved but the other four are in a straight line, though miles apart. The Shawnee

---

[1] If this date is correct, then these were the "plundering" vikings - not the Norse Christians.

Stone may originally have also been part of the straight line. Dr. Nielsen believed the characters could have been chiseled before 800 A.D. The transcriptions on all five rocks are from the oldest 24 rune alphabet used in Scandinavia between 300 and 800 A.D.[1]

We should mention that Dr. Lee Woodward, a minster, has written a book proclaiming the rock to be "a secret La Salle Monument and Historical Marker". It is his theory that the letters were carved between 1687 and 1688 by Gemme Hiens, a German-English companion of La Salle, the French explorer. He translates the characters to include the birth and death dates of La Salle, who was killed on the Poteau River.

It is significant that since the archeological find of a Viking (Norse) village in Newfoundland in 1960, the number of books and articles questioning the authenticity of the Kensington Runestone has diminished to almost none. On the other had the number of books and articles supporting the legitimacy of the runestone has increased significantly.

Among the more recent books supporting the authenticity of the Kensington Runestone is a book entitled "The Kensington Runestone, Its Place in History" by Thomas E. Reiersgord, published in 2001. The author devoted most of his adult life to researching the question and has concluded that the inscription on the stone was, indeed, carved by Vikings (Norse) in 1362.

Reiersgord concluded that the Vikings (Norse) began their journey at Vinland, which he speculates was located on Anticosti Island off the coast of Labrador. He suggests a couple of possible routes to Lakes Huron and Superior, and that from Lake Superior they worked their way inland to Mille Lacs Lake. He further theorizes that the Vikings (Norse) were helped and guided in their journey by friendly Indians, including the Sioux, who at that time had a major population center at Mille Lacs. He believes that the stone was carried by the Sioux to the Kensington area where they buried it. Reiersgord hypothesizes that the stone was actually carved on an island in Knife Lake (About 18 miles southeast of Mille Lacs) and that the two "skerries" (rocky islands) referred to on the runestone as "landmarks" are the rocky islands on Mille Lacs Lake. The author gives us a new interpretation to the reference on the stone of the Vikings (Norse) returning from fishing and finding "ten men red with blood and dead". Most students of the Kensington Runestone took this to mean they had been killed by

---

[1] If this date is correct, then these were the "plundering" vikings – not the Norse Christians.

Indians. Reiersgord believes the men died from the "Black Death" or Bubonic Plague, the same as killed millions in Europe in the 14th Century. Many victims of the plague discharged large amounts of blood as they died.

The above paragraph is a very brief summary of Reiersgord's theories regarding the runestone. The reader is encouraged to read his book in which he goes into great detail describing the evidence supporting his conclusions. It is very difficult to read the book and not agree with its author.[1]

Scott Wolter and Richard Nielsen have published a new book (2005) entitled "The Kensington Rune Stone, Compelling New Evidence", which also strongly supports the authenticity of the stone. they submit geological evidence that the stone is, indeed, as old as the inscription says it is. Furthermore, The nay-sayers have held that the Swedish runes inscribed on the stone are not of that period. The authors, however, have discovered a connection to previously undeciphered runes found in Swedish graveyards. They have also suggested a decoding of the strange, but deliberate, anomalies in several significant runes. The book is well worth reading and is available on the following website: *http://www.outernetpublishing.com/krs.htm*.

In case you have forgotten the distinction we made at the start of this chapter between "Vikings" and "Norse", the former were the aggressive, plundering Scandinavians who were active into the 11th Century, while the Norse were the more civilized, Catholic Christians who had roots in Norway, Iceland and Greenland and who had short-lived colonies on the east coast of North America. Swedes and Danes were sometimes a part of Norse settlements and expeditions. Because the term "Vikings" is so commonly used to describe both, we have chosen to identify the earlier group as "Vikings" but have added the descriptor "Norse" in parentheses to identify the Christians who followed.[2]

The Kensington Runestone is on display at the Runestone Museum in Alexandria, Minnesota (phone 320-763-3160; www.runestonemuseum.org). It was found 20 miles southwest, near Kensington. The site is now a county park.

---

[1] Reiersgord's book is available for $20 from Al Seltz, 924 E. Mount Faith Ave., Fergus Falls, MN 56537-2330

[2] A book by Else Roesdahl, "Vikings", gives the date 1066 as the time of the last major Viking barbaric, plundering expedition (to England).

So Why Did Chief Ongewae Have Curly Hair?

Ongewae, an Ojibway man of the Marten Clan.
Charles Bird King painted this portrait of the
Ojibway leader in 1827. The painting was published
as a lithograph in McKenney and Hall, *Indian Tribes
of North America*. Note the curly hair and
European facial features.

Chief Hole-In-the-Day
the younger of Gull Lake. Note the
European facial features.

Ongewae was a chief of the Fond du Lac Ojibwe. He posed for the portrait shown here in 1827; it was painted by Charles Bird King. Not only does the chief have curly hair, but his facial features are strikingly European.

Then there was Chief Curly Head of the Gull Lake Ojibwe; he moved his village there in 1800 from Sandy Lake. There were no cameras at that early date and, unfortunately, if he was painted or sketched, that art did not survive, but the odds are very strong there was good reason to call him "Curly Head"!

Lastly, I have seen Minnesota Ojibwe men who are alive today who also have curly hair, although they are not common. The point is, nearly all American Indians of all tribes have very straight hair, so where does the curly hair come from? In the case of modern day Ojibwe, it is possible they have recent white ancestors, but not so with the two chiefs.

William Warren in his "History of the Ojibway" (1885) tells us that according to oral tradition, the Ojibwe lived on the east coast of North America for several hundreds of years before migrating west on both sides of the Great Lakes, settling in the sixteen and seventeen hundreds in Wisconsin, Minnesota and north across the border into Canada.

Thomas Peacock and Marlene Wisuri are more specific in a more recent publication, "We Look In All Directions" (2002), saying that when the Ojibwe were on the East Coast they were pretty much concentrated in what is now Newfoundland.

Thomas Reiersgord in his book, "The Kensington Runestone, Its Place In History" (2001), reminds us that the remains of a Viking village was discovered in 1960 in Newfoundland. It is very likely that the Ojibwe were living in that region at that time. It is also likely that other Viking settlements existed in this Ojibwe territory (around 1000 A.D.). Reiersgord theorizes that the famous Viking village known as "Vinland" was located on Anticosti Island[1], which would also have been Ojibwe territory at that time.

Although the Viking Sagas recorded considerable fighting with the local natives, there were also times of peace and it is surely within the realm of possibility that there was some inter-marrying between the two races. And we do know that many Scandinavians have curly hair!

William Warren ("History of the Ojibway") listed 21 different totems or clans of Ojibwe; each was named for an animal or bird. He also said that eighty percent of the Ojibwe were in six of the 21 totems or clans. Among the six largest clans was the Marten Totem. We know that Chief Ongewae of Fond du Lac was a member of the Marten Totem because the portrait artist included a marten in the picture. When the white settlers first met the Ojibwe in Minnesota, Wisconsin and Canada, they probably noticed that the members of the Marten Totem (who were mainly in Minnesota) had European features and some had curly hair. Because the Ojibwe insisted that people marry outside their clan (the man chose a wife from another clan), the European features, including curly hair, are now shared with other totems. We do have photographs (page 88) and paintings of Hole in the Day the Younger of Gull Lake who does have European features. It may or may not have any significance that he liked to dress half in Indian and half in white man's clothing. Since his father, Hole in the Day the Elder, originally came from near Lake Superior, it is likely that he was of the Marten Totem.

DNA tests have been perfected to the point where individuals can learn from which nationalities or regions of the world their ancestors came. It has become quite popular for black Americans to discover with which tribe or nation in Africa their ancestors were associated. The tests, at this writing, are not cheap. They range between $100 and $400. Because they are so long removed from their original homeland, Native

---

[1] Reiersgord came to this conclusion because of all the grapes found there.

Americans find the cost in the higher range. The day may be near when we will learn the original homelands of the various North American tribes of Indians. Such studies may be a good use for casino profits!

Reiersgord reports that, "a 1998 study at the Center of Molecular Medicine at Emory University Medical School showed that the Ojibwe Indians in the Great Lake region carry Mitochondrial DNA markers revealing significant European pre-Columbian contact through the maternal line."

Warren, Reiersgord and other students of the Ojibwe cite another piece of evidence that the tribe had pre-Columbian contact with Europeans, namely that Ojibwe oral history speaks of the creation, the flood, and other events that closely parallel the stories of the Old Testament. The Ojibwe also believe in God; they call Him "Kitchi Manito" (the Great Spirit). Many scholars of the 1800s, including Warren and followers of the Mormon Faith, were confident the Ojibwe were members of one of the "lost tribes of Israel[1]." Reiersgord hypothesizes that the reason the Ojibwe were forbidden to marry within their totem was the result of their contacts with the Vikings who were forbidden by their religion to marry cousins.

As another example of pre-Columbian European impact on the Ojibwe, Reiersgord suggests that there are striking similarities between the Masonic Lodge and the Midewiwin Society of the Minnesota and Wisconsin Ojibwe, and that those similarities were in place long before whites came into this region. He cites the following similarities[2]:

1. A cross is the symbol of the 4th degree of the Midewiwin Society.

2. The rituals and ceremonies of the Midewiwin Society's 4th degree is very much like the 3rd degree of the Masonic Lodge.

3. In both societies, candidates for degrees must make payments.

4. There are mystical aspects to the ceremonies of both.

5. Both have an organized "priesthood".

William Warren, writing more than 100 years earlier, also compared the Midewiwin Society to the Masonic Lodge, but doesn't explain how he reached that conclusion. Several modern day scholars agree, however.

---

[1] Some modern day Hebrew scholars now say there were no "lost tribes of Israel".
[2] Reiersgord credited Harold Hickerson, a contemporary scholar, for these comparisons.

OTHER POSSIBLE PRE-COLUMBIAN VISITORS TO NORTH AMERICA
THE KENNEWICK MAN

In 1996, on the banks of the Columbia River, an unusual skeleton was washed out of the mud during a speedboat race. Since the bones were identified as being about 9000 years old, the "Caucasiod-like" scull aroused all kinds of speculation. However, before scientists had the opportunity to fully examine the relics, Indian tribes demanded that the bones be given a respectful burial immediately. They were

Restored image of the
Kennewick man.

supported by the Department of Interior. While the case was being considered by the courts the skeleton was placed in safe keeping where it could not be examined further and the government buried the discovery site under two million pounds of dirt. A federal magistrate ruled in 2002 that scientists could examine the bones before burial and that decision was upheld by an appeals court in 2004.

Since the ruling, eleven scientists have been busy examining the remains. At this writing it has been determined that the unusually shaped scull most resembles that of an Ainu, and ethnic minority in Japan – but that decision may not be final.

HOW DID THE ANCESTORS OF
INDIANS GET HERE?

Most Indian tribes ascribe to the theory that they originated in North America and have been here since the beginning of time, which disagrees with a long accepted theory that these first Americans migrated across a temporary land bridge between Siberia and Alaska about 12,000 years ago. It has also been assumed that these new Americans worked their way south across country. Recent discoveries by Canadians of artifacts on the bottom of the ocean along the west coast - starting with Alaska – have given rise to a new theory that the immigrants followed the west coast as they worked their way south. During the glacial ages, the ocean dropped more than 50 feet. Artifacts, such as fire rings and ashes, have been found under water, indicating that the immigrants followed the shore (now submerged) on their journey south.

THE IRISH?

A large, round boulder discovered near the L'Anse aux Meadows Viking village site bears unusual and very old letters and markings that resemble most the medieval alphabet used by the Irish. This one finding hardly justifies concluding that Irish pre-Columbian explorers were in North America, but it is a start!

THE PHOENICIANS?

The Phoenicians were known for their extensive travel so it is not surprising that unusual carvings or markings that don't seem to fit any other explanation are sometimes described as possibly of that origin. It has been suggested that extensive copper mining in the Lake Superior region was the work of Phoenicians and that the copper was used by them to make bronze.

THE HEBREW?

The Ten Commandments have been inscribed in old Hebrew on a rock tablet found near Las Lunas, New Mexico. Has one of the "Lost Tribes of Israel" been found?

SOUTH AMERICA

Although our focus is on North America, it is of interest that a Chinese scholar, Mike Xu, insists that carved stone blades found in Guatemala are "distinctly of Chinese origin" and may be dated approximately 1000 B.C. Chinese legends also tell of explorations to South America by their huge, pre-Columbian cargo ships.

The scull of a young woman found in Brazil is thought to be 11,600 years old and to have Negroid characteristics.

CONCLUSION

What I have written in these last pages is mostly speculation, but taken together with the documentation of all the previous pages, we can safely conclude that the Welch, Vikings and Norse were in North America long before Christopher Columbus.

We are still struggling to understand where all the so-called Native American tribes originated. They came to North America thousands of years before the whites. Maybe DNA testing will give us the answers. I wish that we knew enough now to make that the subject of my next book!

ADDENDUM

I have placed this next document in the addendum rather than in the main text of the book because it probably does not refer to Europeans on the continent before Columbus – yet it might. The presenter, George Stuntz, speaks of ample evidence that "a race of people" occupied northeastern Minnesota, northwestern Wisconsin, and adjacent Canada "in a very remote age". As you will read from the following document, Stuntz cites three major pieces of evidence:

1. Ancient evidences of mining a variety of ores and metals long before the Indians who inhabited the area at the time the first whites arrived.

2. Several rivers and streams had been damned with huge boulders to provide channels deep enough to float the boats that carried whatever was mined.

3. Trees not native to the area had been planted in groves, including oaks (the acorns were ground into flour), maple (for the sap and sugar), plum (for their fruit) and Linden (to provide fibrous bark from which they could make twine, fish nets, etc.).

Schunts does not mention the copper mines on islands in Lake Superior. Although it is known that more recent tribes of Indians worked these mines, there is a school of thought that there was far more copper mined than could have been used by neighboring Indians and therefore they could possibly have been mined by Europeans, such as the Phoenicians, who were believed to have ventured beyond their Mediterranean base and used copper to manufacture bronze. Nevertheless, it is my best guess (and only a guess) that the early race of people to which Stuntz refers were Indians.

The earliest inhabitants of this area who have been identified with a name are the "Laurel People", best known for their huge burial mounds. Exploration of one of the mounds found skeletons of a people six feet in height – very tall for people anywhere in the world in that day. If the Laurel people were not Indians, then who were they? We do not know what happened to the Laurel people.

So, who was this George Stuntz? If you wish to check the internet you will find that he was a surveyor and prospector who worked for both governmental and private interests. Several years after making the following presentation to the Minnesota Academy of Natural Sciences, he became president of that organization.

I am indebted to my friend, Dan Seekins, Staples, Minnesota, for providing me with the transcript which follows:

"EVIDENCES OF EARLY MAN IN NORTHEASTERN MINNESOTA
BY GEORGE R. STUNTZ

(READ BY HIM ON DECEMBER 2, 1884 BEFORE THE MINNESOTA ACADEMY OF NATURAL SCIENCES)

Forty years of my life have been spent in prosecuting the public land surveys of the government. My field of operation has been on both sides of the Mississippi River from the northern boundary of Missouri to the international boundary on Rainy Lake. I could only read as I ran over the surfaces of the country undisturned by modern civilization.

The facts in my possession I give you, perhaps some conclusions. These last you can take for what they are worth.

Some months since the Rev,. Dr, J. H. Tuttle of your city gave us in Duluth a very interesting lecture in which, mixed up with incidents of travel, he gave us stereopticon views of ruins, some of which have a record of over forty centuries. And in that connection, he remarked that America had no ruins unless the mounds and tumuli of the Mississippi Valley could give us a clue to its former inhabitants.

That these earth works have a history and one of a very interesting character and that a race of people occupied that country in a very remote age and that their colonies penetrated the regions in the northeastern portions, not only of this state but of Canada, we have plenty of evidence. In the north, mounds do not occur so frequently but always occupy a sightly position near some natural highway of travel, or on some locality near a lake having the best food supply the country afforded.

They did not live entirely by the chase but cultivated the land. They introduced and cultivated certain fruits. They planted and protected certain forest trees such as the oak, the Sugar Maple and the Linden in regions far beyond where they are indigenous. These forest trees growing as they do in isolated orchards in the extreme northeastern portion of the state, a mountainous, rocky region, stripped of alluvial soil by the stupendous glaciers of two glacial periods, the mountains crumbled to fragments, a debris scattered for hundreds of miles to the south and west, forming the drift hills and alluvial or partially alluvial Jack Pine sandy plains of Wisconsin and Minnesota, could hardly have their seeds scattered to the north by any ocean currents, or up streams against the currents of rivers. It hardly seems possible that the seeds of these trees could have been brought from the north and survived the terrible abrasion of centuries of glacial action.

They are all essential for the wants of a half civilized people – the acorns for food, the sugar for diet in connection with the rice and corn they cultivated and the bark of the Linden for cordage and twine and in the manufacture of nets and mats.

The alluvial lands in the Mississippi Valley, as evidenced by the extensive mounds and numerous tumuli supported a large population. These people penetrated the north and in the ascent of rivers, obstructed by rapids of bowlders and by broad shallow channels, they began to leave monuments of their skills as engineers. Nearly or quite all the streams leading from the Mississippi and Lake Superior to the north and into the Rainy Lake region have been improved by some former race possessing more mechanical skill than the Indians now residing there.

Those ancient mound builders, for such we will assume these prehistoric voyageurs to be, had two or three important routes from the Mississippi to Lake Superior. The St. Croix River route through Wisconsin was the nearest and most used and at Yellow Lake are extensive earth works and tumuli. One mount on the shore of that lake measures about 19 feet in height and is seventy-one paces in circumference. It occupies a sightly locality. Pottery and ornaments common to these people are found in these mounds. A few miles further up the river the line of travel diverged into the Brule River and thence down to Lake Superior. The second route by water was up the Eau Claire through Lake Superior. From the mouth of Bad river an extensive copper region on Keweenaw Point was easily reached.

The third and shorter route was over a long portage to the mouth of Sioux River, southwest of Bayfield.

The way stations of the food supply of these routes of travel are about 100 miles apart, a three to four day trip. At Bayfield and Ashland, the great fish supply was reached. At Ontanagon, Eagle River and Portage Lake these people mined large amounts of copper and exported it over the routes mentioned to the extensive markets in the lower Mississippi Valley.

To the country north of Lake Superior there were different routes. The most important one was up the Mississippi to Sandy Lake, thence across the divide to the St. Louis River (Gichi Gummi Sibi of the Chippewas, I.E., River of the Great Lake). From the mouth of East Savannah the combined route from the Mississippi and from Lake Superior continued up the St. Louis and its northerly branch, the Embarrass River, to and across the great water shed of the Mesabi Mountains, then down the Pike River into Lake Vermilion. This was the great route from the Mississippi Valley to the mining regions of northeastern Minnesota. Farther up the Mississippi there lay an important route from Lake Winnebigoshish to and through Bowstring Lake and its extensive wild rice fields, down Big fork River to Rainy River and then on to the great waterway extending along the international boundary for two hundred miles.

On this route the principal town or stopping place was at White Oak Point as ancient mounds and fragments of pottery attest. Another important route from Lake Superior was up Pigeon River to its source; thence across the height of land down the valley of Rainy Lake and River to the Lake of the Woods.

There were other lines of travel of minor importance leading into that country, but I have described enough of them to show that the country was occupied. The inhabitants were a mining people, and in order to get the products of their mines to the great populous centers they had to improve the rivers enumerated above, so far as to accommodate their light draft boats. This they have done, and in such a manner as to reduce the transport to the shortest possible distance. Slight dams were built to flood shoals and jetties to direct the water from bank to bank, so as to secure a sufficient depth to float their craft. I am not aware of any relics or works to indicate that they used beasts of burden or any mode of land transportation save packing on men's backs.

The St. Louis River falls about 600 feet from the mouth of the Cloquet River to Fond du Lac, at the level of Lake Superior. The distance by the stream is about 24 miles. This section of the river is exceedingly rough. There are some reasons for believing that at Pine Island, 3 miles above Knife Falls, the rapids are artificial or partially so – on the Grand Rapids 5 miles above and at their head, a dike of bowlders of enormous size, so compactly placed and sloping down stream at such an angle as to revert the force of the highest floods. This dam floods the stream 4 miles to the mouth of the Cloquet River. About 4 miles, just below the mouth of this last stream, a dam composed of heavy rocks, all rounded bowlders is thrown at right angles across the river of sufficient height (about 7 feet) to flood the stream above for 12 miles. Throughout this whole distance the scarcity of bowlders in the stream and on the banks would indicate that they had all been removed and placed in that dam.

Two more of those dams occur in Town 51, Ranges 18 and 19, and farther up the river at a point 3 1/2 miles above Whitefish, at Swan River rapids and at Cedar rapids. But the most marked improvements are on the Embarrass River above Eshquagama Lake. This stream is the most northerly branch of the St. Louis River. It makes a cut through the Mesabi Mountains which rise in Town 59, Range 15, to a height above the valley on each side of the stream of from 600 to 800 feet in the distance of half a mile. But the nature of this channel is now visible at a few points between the seven artificial lakes that have been made by dams of bowlders thrown across the valley making the 12 miles of the river from the Eshquagama or lowest lake to Wine Portage with its five portages the easiest part of the canoe route from Duluth to Vermilion Lake. At the crossing of the wagon road at the bridge that the heaviest spring floods cannot move them from the grade they are placed at. This dam formerly held the water three feet higher than at present and is about 100 feet long on the south side of the river. It has been lowered laterally to allow canoes to pass without making portage, and this lowering of the dam has been a damage to the navigation on two shoals between lakes above. I cannot leave this locality without calling attention to some facts that would seem to indicate that quite a settlement of these people resided in the vicinity of these lakes.

On the south side of Eshquagama Lake, about forty rods from the shore, situated on a sand plain is a mound about twenty feet in diameter and seven feet high. On this mound is a thick growth of Jack Pine.

About two miles northeast of this mound opposite the third lake is a grove of plum bushes, ancient Burr Oak trees, Lindens and Elms growing on the upland. There are no other trees of these species on the uplands in the whole region.

The prevailing timber is Coniferous, mixed with White Birch and Aspen Poplar. If these lakes are artificial, the construction of the necessary dams would have required a large number of workman a term of years. At Wine Portage the stream falls 36 feet over a dam of bowlders. In season of high water these rapids can be run by canoes coming down stream. The fall is about 6 feet in a hundred for 600 feet. At this point the channel is straight; another evidence that it was constructed to canoe in a crooked channel where the craft was moving at a rate of speed equal to a railroad train. At the upper end of the portage the dam was raised high enough to flood the water back for nine miles up the valley to a point where the Iron Range Railroad crosses the stream. The lake thus formed covered from 10,000 to 15,000 acres of land, and has been maintained so long that it is filled with a vegetable deposit, peat bearing on its surface Spruce and Tamarack trees, Cranberries and the peat mosses. This lake is connected with a similar one, created by a dam on Pike River, which like the first is filled with peat. The depth of peat in this swamp may give us dates from which to calculate the period of time that has elapsed since the valley was flooded. Assuming the deposit to be six feet deep and that it accumulated at the rate of one inch in a hundred years, we have a period of 7,200 years.

After passing the divide we reach Pike River, a stream only about two rods wide in Town 60, Range 15. This stream empties into Vermilion Lake, it has four dams on it below the one spoken of above. I will describe two of them.

The first, at the crossing of the wagon road from Duluth to Lake Vermilion in Town 61, Range 15. At this point a dam of bowlders has been placed across the valley, the largest of which are several tons weight each. These rocks have been taken from the bed of the stream above. The height of the dam does not exceed four feet, yet it makes the stream navigable for nine miles. When we consider that this country in the valley of Vermilion Lake is perfectly paved with rocks, torn from ledges during the glacial period, that these rocks occupy the hill tops, and that in the excavation of the valley, of a stream having a grade of less than six feet to the mile, a stream of great volume would not even move small pebbles, nor have they the slightest action on sand, we should expect that the removal of the finer clays and sands would give more prominence to the bowlders. Here we find a stream running through just such a valley as I have mentioned and for nine miles one can move along in an average stage of water on a placid canal. I conclude therefore that the channel has been closed and the rocks piled into these dams. About one-fourth of a mile above Vermilion Lake the streams falls over a ledge of altered slates. Above these falls, there is a rapid 500 feet in length in which distance the stream falls about 12 feet. At the head of this rapid, the stream suddenly deepens to 10 feet and so abruptly that the stones appear to have been laid up in the form of a well. For the distance of about 1500 feet above this dam the stream crosses ledges of trap rocks and then opens out into a valley flooded for six miles and a half or so to the foot of the next rapids. If the boulders were removed from the channel above the falls, the stream would drain the valley and destroy the navigation of the stream for canoes for a mile and one-half.

Vermilion Lake. The extensive interior lake is thirty miles long. It is divided into bays by long capes and is studded with numerous islands, varying in size from a few rods to several miles in length and is diversified in beauty as they are in size. The present every tint of green and with the surrounding hills, they present a landscape seldom surpassed in beauty. On the shores of such a lake, with its abundant supply of fish for food, we are naturally let to look for traces of settlements of this ancient people, and they are there. The whole region north of the Mesabi mountains is covered with bowlders so thickly scattered over the surface, that it is hardly possible to drive a team without first clearing the track. It is Nicollet's "land of rocks and water". The first evidence of improved land that we get is on a cape about a half mile east of the mouth of Pike River. Although the area is small, it is very evident it has been cleared of stones and cultivated. Here grow the Oak, the Linden and the Plum, or they were growing there eighteen years ago, before extensive forest fires destroyed the timber around the shores of the lake. Farther east in Section 25, Town 62, Range 16, is an island of not more than two scores in extent with similar indications; at the mouth of Two Rivers lies a spot now occupied by the Minnesota Iron Company and cultivated as a farm and garden. Eighteen years ago, it was covered with a dense forest; successive fires destroyed the timber and the company plowed a large area without being troubled by stones. I claim that there is no locality on this lake where this can be done unless the boulders are first removed, and if the have been removed it has been done by human labor, and it was not done by the Indians at present inhabiting the region. Until quite recently these Indians knew nothing about farming and lived entirely by hunting and fishing and by gathering the berries and wild rice of the region. At Sucker Bay, on a cape in Section 23 and 24, town 62, Range 16, the present Indian farm is quite an extensive tract, now cultivated by the Indians under the direction of a government farmer. Advantage was taken of this favorable locality because the stones had been cleared off. Here we find additional evidence of presence of the Mound Builder, in fragments of pottery which have the marks and the general appearance of similar fragments found in the mounds at Yellow Lake in Wisconsin, and at White Oak Point on the Upper Mississippi, in Itasca County. There are several other localities on the lake that show signs of similar improvements and the planting of Oaks, Lindens, Elms and Plum trees.

The query naturally arises: What induced these people to occupy these northern regions. Could it have been the summer resort of a people who admired the beautiful scenery and the excellent food supply – the fish, rice and the game? It hardly seems possible that they would devote time and labor in improving these rivers if they did not have something more weighty to transport than ordinary baggage or provisions. the indications are that they were miners and came here to work the mineral deposits, and that these improvements on the streams were made to transport their products to a southern market.

On the north side of the bluff in Section 27, town 62, Range 15, is an excavation made in solid jasper, one of the hardest rocks known, and exceedingly tough and consequently difficult to break. The depth of this cut is not known, as the sides have given way and the pit is partially filled. Here masses of rock, from three to ten cubic yards in size, have been detached and removed out of the cut to the dump. There are no marks to indicate how these immense blocks of jasper were detached, or what mechanical appliances were used to hoist them out of the cut and place them on the banks. There are evidences that fire was used in working certain portions of the rock; in the dump pile fragments of charcoal and ashes are quite frequently found. A gravel walk is still visible and in tolerable repair, leading from the cut to the dump. This evidently was built for carrying out the materials of the mine. An examination of the bluff a short distance to the east of this cut disclosed a slate vein, carrying a notable quantity of a yellow and red ocher. This may have been the material for which the mining was done; whatever it was, the vein has been worked to the westward for the distance of several hundred feet across a flat, and to a depth below water level. For 200 miles to the eastward, along the international boundary, are improved river courses and ancient diggings, requiring a vast

amount of labor and leaving monuments in stone of the patience, skill and industry of this ancient people.

I regret that I have not time to describe localities farther to the eastward or to
enlarge on the engineering skill displayed in the construction of the stone dams.
They effectually stop or hold the water at a given height in its low stages, and let it
down an easy grade over a wide expanse in time of floods.

I conclude that this semi-civilized people cultivated the soil, they planted and
cultivated certain forest and fruit trees, they cultivated the wild rice, they understood pisciculture and stocked the interior lakes and lived largely on a fish diet,
they improved the navigation of rivers leaving lasting monuments of their engineering skill, and they worked the mines for ocher or paints, for the precious metals and for copper.

America has ruins; America has a history; but it must be read in the footprints
of this ancient people."

SELECTED BIBLIOGRAPHY*

Belgen, Theodore, *The Kensington Ruenstone*,
Minnesota Historical Society, 1968

Canadian National Parks Website

Catlin, George, *North Amercian Indians, Volumes I and II*, 1854

DeCosta, Ben, *The Pre-Columbian Discovery of America by the Northmen*,
J. Muncel, 1868

De Roo, P., *History of America Before Columbus, Volumes I and II*,
J. P. Lippincot, 1900

Journals of Lew and Clark, Houghton and Mifflin, 1953

Kensington Runestone Website

Lewis, Thomas and Kneberg, Madeline, *Tribes taht Slumber*,
University of Tennessee Press, 1958

D. Lund, Lake of the Woods, Earliest Accounts,
Adventure Pub., Cambridge, MN, 1984

D. Lund, *Lake of the Woods, Yesterday and Today*,
Adventure Pub., Cambridge, MN 1975

McMahan, Basil, *The mystery of the Old Stone Fort*, Nashville,
Tennessee Book Co., 1965

Peacock, Thomas and Wisuri, Marlene, *We Look in All Directions*,
Afton H.S. Press, 2002

Pugh, Ellen, *Bravce His Soul (Prince Madoc)*,
Dodd, Meade and Co., 1920

Reiersgord, Thomas, *The Kensington Ruenstone, It's Place in History*, 2001

Warren, William, *A History of the Ojibway*, 1885

Young, Bennett, *The Prehistoric Men of History*,
J.P. Morton and Co., 1910

*The above references were most helpful, although more than a hundred books, articles and Websites were studied.